The Schools That Fear Built

SEGREGATIONIST ACADEMIES IN THE SOUTH

The Schools That Fear Built

DAVID NEVIN AND ROBERT E. BILLS

Introduction by Terry Sanford, President, Duke University

Published by **ACROPOLIS BOOKS LTD.** • WASHINGTON, D.C. 20009

ACROPOLIS BOOKS
Colortone Building, 2400 17th St., N.W.
Washington, D.C. 20009

Printed in the United States of America by
COLORTONE PRESS, Creative Graphics Inc.
Washington, D.C. 20009

Library of Congress Catalog Number 76-27582
ISBN: 0-87491-177-4   (cloth)
ISBN: 0-87491-179-6   (paper)

CONTENTS

Part II: The Analysis
        By Robert E. Bills

Preface

The Schools that Fear Built constitutes the first full discussion ever published on the new private schools that have sprung up across the South in the wake of integration orders—the schools known as segregationist academies. It is the result of a study undertaken by the Lamar Society, a group of progressive southerners interested in improving their society. Because the Lamar Society's interest is the South, it limited its study to segregationist academies in the South, but there is ample evidence that the phenomenon described is national rather than regional. Segregationist academies exist in Boston and Detroit and Los Angeles in forms and with motives and outlooks that make them virtually indistinguishable from those in the South.

The Society's project began as part of its Task Force on Public Education when public school superintendents attending its annual meeting at Jackson, Mississippi in 1973 asked for assistance in getting a grasp on the new schools which then were erupting all over the South. The Society asked the Ford Foundation for the funding of this undertaking and received a grant making possible two years of effort.

The Society's project went well beyond that study of private schools which is this book's subject. It also examined conditions that follow major school integration orders and began developing programs to help communities deal with the resulting turmoil, of which the sudden opening of private segregationist academies is likely to be just one example. This community action effort was focused in Louisville, Kentucky; eventually it led a major project which is offering a wide variety of information and expert assistance in dealing with desegregation tension to a number of American cities.

The Schools that Fear Built is divided into two parts. They were done separately and by different authors. The first part is a qualitative report designed to present a clear and graphic picture of the nature of the new schools.

The second part is a study of eleven particular schools conducted by a sophisticated researcher in education and supported by computer analysis of test results. Both studies were conducted under the auspices of the Society's project. It is interesting and indicative that the two reports, though their approach was opposite, arrived at similar conclusions. Thus the two parts form a well integrated whole, taking the new schools both from a broad overall viewpoint and a controlled, specific viewpoint, so that each part enhances and supports the other.

The people who operate the new schools have welcomed the attention. The Society's project members made it plain that their bias was toward support of public schools and against trends that hurt public schools. The operators of the new schools feel quite the opposite, but only rarely did that interfere with an interview. The new school people are proud of what they are doing and enjoy talking about it.

Part One was written by David Nevin, a national journalist and author of various books, and is based on the project's research. Staff members of the Lamar Society made many field visits to the new schools and to other public and private educational agencies. Staff members included the Society's president, Dr. Frank A. Rose, Dr. A.W. Braden, Mardi Osman and Mr. Nevin. Dr. Rose dealt extensively with southern accrediting agencies, state departments of education and southern political leaders concerned with the new school phenomenon, and made field trips to schools and organizations supporting new schools. Dr. Braden's background in education, the humanities and theology contributed to the philosophic understanding as well as to the assessment of the schools, many of which he visited in both rural and urban parts of the South. Ms. Osman served as coordinator of the Louisville Consensus Committee, conducted research in many state departments of education and visited classrooms of private academies. Dr. Houston Conley, Professor, Virginia Polytechnic Institute, played a major role in Louisville and participated in many conferences on the problems caused by segregated academies. Persons serving in an advisory or consultative role included Richard B. Fields, then of the University of Tennessee Law School, and who first called to the attention of the Society these academies; Hayes Mizell of the American Friends Service Committee; and Mrs. June Key of Louisville. Journalists Neal R. Peirce and Reese Cleghorn, John Freeman, Superintendent of Schools at Memphis, and Samuel B. Ethridge of the National Education Association, participated in a Society symposium on the subject.

Mrs. Beth Tanner typed many research reports, maintained all files and records, and typed the manuscript for this book.

Part II was written by Robert E. Bills, a Research Professor of Education at the University of Alabama, who conducted the research on which it is based. The University of Alabama made an important contribution to the work by making it possible for Dr. Bills to conduct his study of eleven particular schools. Dr. Bills has been a high school teacher and Professor of Education and of Educational Psychology, Assistant Dean for Research in Education of the College of Education at the University of Alabama and dean of the college. As a high school teacher, he was troubled by the personal problems that children presented and the difficulty that teachers had in responding. In pursuit of this interest, he became a clinical psychologist and began developing the theories on the affective side of school life and the system for assessing them that have become his life work. In 1975, the University of Alabama Press published his *A System for Assessing Affectivity*. Among other things, it describes the procedures and instruments he developed to measure qualities which contribute to a whole and an intelligently behaving person in the classroom. Dr. Bills gave his instruments to students in the eleven schools and at the same time cast an experienced schoolman's eye on them and their operations. He included his resulting assessment in his report. Dr. Bills had the assistance of Dr. Lewis Blackwell, Professor of Educational Psychology, and four graduate assistants in the College of Education. They were Angel Antonio Marquez, Charles Minder, Wayne Moffett and Dennis Barbakow. The University also allowed the use of extensive computer time for the analysis of the data gathered at the schools.

The overall effort received considerable help from the Legal Defense Fund, the Southern Regional Council, staff members of the Southern Association of Colleges and Secondary Schools and the Lawyer's Committee for Civil Rights Under Law.

Special appreciation is expressed to Dr. Robert Saunders, Dean of the School of Education, Memphis State University.

As noted above, the entire project was funded by a grant from the Ford Foundation, and the Society is deeply grateful to the Foundation for making the work possible. In addition, the authors are grateful for the ideas, encouragement and support they received from the Foundation's officers, especially Harold Howe II, Edward J. Meade Jr., and Ralph G. Bohrson.

Introduction:
Portent and Opportunity

By Terry Sanford,
President, Duke University

More than the morning dew has visited the South in the last two decades. During that time a host of private schools or academies, usually known as Christian or segregationist, depending on one's perspective, have been established. Some of these have had life spans not much longer than a dewdrop's, while others are appearing to become permanent fixtures in our society. There is a great deal yet to be learned about these academies, and from them, and this work by the Lamar Society is a valuable effort toward that end.

That so many of these very similar institutions appeared almost simultaneously indicates that the clouds from which they coalesced had been forming for some time. One such cloud began gathering in the 17th century, with the slave trade, and that ever lengthening shadow has not yet dissipated. It might be held that the true dimensions of racial disharmony in this country, which had been submerged for many years, resurfaced with the issue of integration in the public schools.

And other clouds had formed. Some of our national undertakings had begun increasingly to be called into question—by the civil rights movement and the Vietnam War demonstrations among other things. The Supreme Court decision seeming to remove prayer from the schools thus was regarded by many, not as an effort to maintain constitutional separation of church and state, but as another attack on our historic and national values.

These academies are in a sense an attempt to deal with these problems by avoiding them. While this might be an acceptable course of action for single institutions, it is not a possible course for society. We must face the problems.

The academies can be seen as an attempt to return to the state of affairs that had developed, quite comfortably for the majority, before the country began to undergo its great period of change and self-doubt. The schools established are closely patterned on the public schools which the parents of the present students remember —white, authoritarian, with strong emphasis on the 3 R's, and usually with healthy doses of religion and the pledge of allegiance thrown in. As is the case with most reactions, they may go even further than the dimly remembered ideal, for there are signs that the academies are if anything more rigid and religious than the public schools of the forties and fifties which they are an attempt to recreate. As such, it should be considered that they might put their students at a disadvantage in the world they will encounter, which most probably will not be anything like the world of thirty years ago.

These academies might also have a broader impact on society than just the influence they have on their students. By removing from the public schools a considerable element of the community, both children and parents, they place an additional burden upon the already staggering public school system. The public schools, however, cannot be seen as blameless. The springing up of these academies is an indictment of the public schools for failing, or appearing to fail, to respond to the needs of an important element of the community, and not solely an immature reaction on the part of disgruntled racists, as some would contend. The fear and distrust of the public schools among those who send their children to academies is eloquently attested by the fact of their paying taxes to support one system of education as well as tuition for the education of their own children. This may be the major lesson of this study.

The operators and patrons of the new schools are proud of their accomplishments. On the other hand, the editors and investigators of this study project admit in advance their bias is "toward support of public schools and against trends that hurt public schools." This is the conflict, and these are the questions. Do these schools provide adequate education, and do they harm the public schools? Will they, on the other hand, become the additional prod that contributes to needed improvement in the public schools?

The study upon which this book is based reveals, among other things, that both students and parents are more satisfied with the academies than their counterparts in the public schools are with their institutions. One reason for this, it is suggested, is that the school community as a whole has more of a sense of involvement because the academies are more responsive to the desires of the parents. This raises a challenge for the public schools, and that may be the more obscure but more significant conclusion to be drawn from the study. If so, the work that went into this study is of great value and well worth the effort.

To whom do the public schools belong if not the public? Why were they seen as so unresponsive that a great many people just pulled out? Race and religion are *certainly important factors here, but it is fair to assume that many people, presently straining the family income to the breaking point to afford an academy education for their children, would be influenced by neither of these if they thought the kind of education and community involvement they want for their children was available in the public schools. There is probably no stronger force in society than the parents' desire to see their children properly educated. That too is one of the study's inescapable conclusions.*

In all fairness it must be admitted that the public schools had placed upon them responsibilities for social change far beyond traditional expectations, and they have consequently neglected or been unable to satisfy many of their patrons. It can be hoped that we have passed beyond the period of transition and disorder, that stability and better education are at hand, and that we will be able to resolve our differences within the framework of public education.

We cannot wish the academies out of existence. Some are undoubtedly here to stay. Others are not yet well established, and their patrons would probably be happy to return to the public schools if they had confidence the public schools could meet their needs. As the study points out, the academies were not the cause of anything, but the result of dislocations and misunderstandings in the society which will only be corrected in time by the goodwill and involvement of all people.

The purpose of any school is the education of young people, and these schools are too numerous to ignore. We can learn from them, we can learn because of them, and perhaps we can build bridges of better communication and understanding. As the problems which surfaced in the last generation begin to be dealt with intelligently, and as we strive to improve our public schools, to restore a sense of community, perhaps we will see a flow back into the public schools which would mark a new public confidence and likely be beneficial to all.

Part One

The Schools That Fear Built

By David Nevin

This section consists of a general examination of the nature of segregationist academies in the South.

1

The Problem

As desegregation of public schools in the South has become a reality in the early and mid 1970s, the number of people turning to private schools to avoid desegregation has grown steadily. The movement to private schools began in the 1960s when the idea of massive resistance to desegregation orders was still current in the South. Today, though desegregation seems generally accepted, the shift to private schools continues.

It is too simple to blame this movement entirely on racism and fear of integration. At a deeper level, it is evidence of a profound division beneath the surface of American society.

It also is true, however, that the growth of the schools has been greatest during the very period when court orders have made southern schools the most desegregated in the nation. The spurts of growth of the new schools can be linked directly to these orders; the schools appear consistently in the wake of integration pressure in the South and have their greatest and often their only major growth in the period when the community is still feeling the shock of the order.

It is no small matter to start a school and it is even more difficult to maintain and stabilize one. So this persistent growth in an education form that is essentially new to the South testifies to the seriousness of those who start them and the parents who support them.

This support is the more significant in view of the historic feeling in the South that private schools were for the rich or those who sought elite status. The average southerner of the past tended to see public schools as the avenue for his hope that his children might escape the economic blight that was the South's condition for so long. Today, many of those same people appear to see private schools in this light. Probably the new schools would not be possible without the new affluence of the South, but it also is true that few of their patrons are rich. Most are middle to lower-middle class working people who pay dearly to support their schools. George and Frances Barton of Memphis, Tennessee, are examples. The Bartons both work in the Firestone tire manufacturing plant there, he as a foreman, she as a secretary, and together they earn just under $20,000 a year. Last year they spent $2,110 to keep their three children in a big Baptist school in Memphis and they expect the cost to rise to about $2,400. The fact that they consider this a bargain testifies to how they feel about the new school movement.

The early segregationist academies were usually secular schools that sprang up on a county-wide basis in rural areas, standing ready to serve any and all white children who applied. The more recent schools and those appearing in the larger cities are almost entirely "Christian" schools, sponsored by an evangelical Protestant church and heavily influenced by the fundamental theology which the more conservative evangelical churches follow. Indeed, as the movement has progressed, the Christian schools have become more and more numerous until today they probably outnumber the older secular academies. But in a larger sense, the difference between them is unimportant, for despite what would seem contrary origins, the schools in practice are so similar as to be indistinguishable. They look the same, are financed in the same ways and from the same motives and teach essentially the same philosophy. Perhaps the single most important point about these schools is their sameness—the homogeneity of student, of teacher, of attitude, of the experience they offer. Across the South the schools vary widely in age, size, wealth, building style—but once you go inside you are in a fixed and unchanging world that hardly varies from school to school or state to state or secular to religious background.

2

The Lamar Society's project was to explore and report on the new schools, not to condemn them, but it would be less than candid not to state the biases that have arisen as the project progressed. Those biases are that the schools are destructive in several ways. The question is not the validity of private education as such, but the effect of these schools and the essentially political as opposed to educational motives that lie behind them. The issue obviously is not the right to start such schools but the wisdom of doing so.

The schools do achieve some of the philosophic impact their patrons consider important, but they also seem destructive:

• To the individual, because despite the schools' claim to the contrary, they offer the student a weak and narrow education that appears inadequate for the modern world.

• To the public schools, because the new schools draw off the students most likely to stabilize and enrich public schools and vitiate the public support that is essential to them.

• To society, because of the damage done public schools and because of the tendency of the new private schools to perpetuate the ignorance and the narrow view of society that long has been the bane of the South.

They also damage the movement toward an integrated society. One of their fundamental purposes is to provide a haven for youngsters fleeing from integrated schools. In metropolitan areas they obviously contribute to—though they do not cause, it should be said clearly—the loss of white students in city schools. Public schools in Memphis, for example, which recently were half white now are little more than a quarter white. Since 1969 public schools in Jackson, Mississippi, have dropped from 54 per cent white to 31 per cent white and private schools have boomed, especially those of the Citizens Council. In specific figures, white enrollment fell from 21,000 to less than 9,000. In some rural areas, particularly in counties in which a majority of the population is black, the new schools have produced resegregation, a return to dual systems, whites in private schools, blacks in public schools.

But it also is true, as their patrons claim, that the reasons for their support go far beyond simple racism. Their success represents a deep conviction on the part of their supporters, which suggests a fundamental and dangerous dissatisfaction in American society.

As the new schools are more evident in the South, so this schism in society may be more endemic there, but both schools and schism are national phenomena. The Society's project has limited itself to the thirteen southern states, but in fact such schools are springing up in many parts of the country. Many are found in California and new ones are appearing in Boston. Overall, the schools' greatest significance may be what they show of a fundamental division in American life.

2

The Ambiguous Numbers

It is impossible to give precise numbers of students now in the segregationist academies of the South. It is possible, however, to make rough estimates which can be supported by figures from a variety of sources.

The difficulty is twofold: first, southern states have notoriously poor means for gathering statistics, and second, the new private schools have philosophical imperatives that lead them to resist the collection of data. The secular academies, after all, were started in protest against trends in public schools, government regulations and specific court orders. It is hard to get them to report to the authority they are resisting.

The increasingly important Christian schools are run by evangelical churches which are independent by nature and as part of their creed. Each church's individual congregation is its own ultimate temporal authority; they report to no central authority as in other faiths. As for reporting to government, they are equally out of tune with the trends of modern society and the government it has produced. Most of the new private schools make some effort to meet minimum state standards, especially in those states which codify and enforce standards. Many of them do report their enrollments with fair regularity. But the point is that enough of them resist reporting to make state figures thoroughly unreliable, and most state departments of education in the South find it politically uncomfortable to press the schools.

The simple fact is that no one monitors the new schools and no one has much statistical material on them.

Neither the state departments nor anyone else has the capacity to search out the schools independently of their own reporting. The schools are usually new. They are intensely local in nature, oriented to their own neighborhood and constituency, neither needing nor wanting any outside participation. Some states require new schools to register, but many do not. Typically the schools start suddenly, often in an aura of righteous hysteria, and they can fold or merge with other schools equally suddenly. It is hard to imagine a survey that would provide precise figures.

Informed estimates are possible, however, and are best seen in relation to the integration orders that have produced such change in the South. After *Brown vs. Board of Education* and the implementing rule in *Brown II* in 1955 ordering desegregation "with all deliberate speed," not much actually happened until the rioting in 1962 at the University of Mississippi over James Meredith's admission. (The integration of Central High School in Little Rock in 1957 which was supported by federal troops attracted wide attention but resulted in little integration.) In 1963 the Fifth Circuit Court took the lead in pressing the region toward compliance with *Brown*, as John Minor Wisdom asserted that "the only school desegregation plan that meets constitutional requirements is one that works." It was obvious that freedom of choice plans were not really working.

In *Green vs. County School Board*, the Supreme Court ruled in 1968 that a Virginia county with only 15 per cent of its black students in integrated schools did not meet the requirements of *Brown*. It placed the burden on the school district to find affirmative means to eliminate segregation, and to turn to other means when freedom of choice was not successful. The effect was to say that all those freedom of choice plans in the South that weren't working were no longer acceptable. The decision also opened the way to the use of percentages as a yardstick to gauge a plan's success. The following year, in *Alexander vs. Holmes County Board of Education*, the court demanded immediate action.

At this point federal district courts, strongly supported by the Fifth Circuit Court, began handing down orders that for the first time produced substantial desegregation in the South. During 1970 and 1971, trends that had been brewing in the South ever since *Brown* suddenly came to pass.

Once the way was cleared, it was relatively easy for courts to devise plans to desegregate small districts that had only a few schools. With the Court's ruling in 1971 in *Swann vs. Charlotte-Mecklenburg Board of Education*, the thrust could shift to larger districts. The case had been tried in 1969 and the district court had devised a plan that included busing to achieve a satisfactory level of integration based on mathematical ratios. Though the Supreme Court included some ambiguous qualifications, in approving *Swann* it specifically approved busing as a tool to achieve integregation and mathematical ratios as an acceptable starting place from which to fashion a plan.

Statistically, Marian Wright Edelman of the Children's Defense League reports, in the eleven years after *Brown*, one percent of black children in the South moved into all-white schools; between 1964-1973 that figure rose to 46 percent.

The growth of private schools in the South closely followed these events. They tended to open only when local whites felt threatened by an integration order. There were only a few at first. In Prince Edward County, Virginia, where public schools were a party to the original *Brown* decision, Prince Edward Academy opened in 1959 and prospers still. But it was 1964 before the Citizens Council, formerly the White Citizens Council, a militant segregationist organization headquartered in Jackson, Mississippi, opened the first of what would become a chain of schools. The first segregationist academies in South Carolina opened in 1964.

Integration was still a token matter, but in those days even tokens alarmed the white communities, particularly in more rural areas. Most of the academies that started in this period were secular because they were an expression of the intentions of all the white people in a district or even a county. Later, when people in larger areas and even major cities faced similar orders, they turned to their churches to provide the organizing locus that in rural areas the geographic county itself provided. The early secular academies were blatantly segregationist. That was their purpose. In rural counties they often became the white school system, with blacks left to the wilting public schools. That remains true in some parts of the South today. In Sumter County, Alabama, for example, Sumter Academy regards itself primarily as a public service and is at pains to help any white child arrange tuition.

At the same time various old-line private schools in the South that had struggled for years to remain solvent now found their enrollment expanding rapidly. With the new students came new resources and new respect for them in their communities. Many such schools announced that they did not wish to be regarded as havens for those fleeing integration, but they grew nevertheless.

Charlotte County Day School, for example, is an old line high quality prep school that had to struggle until *Swann*. Now, though it does not see itself as a haven, it prospers, as do two other good prep schools there, Charlotte Latin and Carmel, both started since *Swann*. In Memphis, Harding Academy, a Church of Christ school, surmounted a long and difficult struggle for existence and now has a system of ten elementary schools feeding a high school, with enrollment of 3,000 and a waiting list of 2,000. This story can be repeated all over the South.

The same is true for some Catholic parochial schools. In some places—as was true in Memphis in the early 1970s—parochial schools valiantly resisted a surge of growth at the expense of public schools. In other places, Catholic schools seem quietly to have opened their doors. This certainly is suggested by their overall enrollment figures.

Catholic schools have been losing enrollment nationally for two decades. In the South, however, Catholic schools have held steady at about 485,000 students. Their failure to shrink in the South can be seen as an equivalent of growth.

As real integration pressure went on in the late 1960s it became evident that private schools of all sorts were providing what amounted to a segregated alternative to integration, whatever their intention. In 1969 before *Alexander*, the Southern Regional Council called attention to the phenomenon and estimated that some 300,000 southern youngsters were in private schools that were segregated in practice. After *Alexander*, in late 1969, it raised the estimate to 400,000. In 1970 it estimated 500,000 and the following year 535,000 students in such schools.

Since then there has been massive integration in urban districts and an eruption of Christian schools in southern cities as well as in rural areas.

In 1970 the departments of education in the thirteen southern states reported a total of 777,561 children in private schools. State officials readily admitted that the figure represented serious under-reporting. The 1970 census, which reached into every household, certainly was more accurate, though given the attitudes of the patrons of private schools, it too can be assumed to be incomplete. The census showed 947,229 children in private schools in the thirteen-state area, or 22 per cent more than the state figures.

In 1975 the departments of education reported a total of 1,012,400 children in private schools. Again it was clear that there was serious under-reporting. There is not a census figure for 1975, of course, but it seems a fair assumption that the percentage by which figures were under-reported in 1970 would still hold in 1975. Increasing the state figure by 22 per cent suggests a total of some 1,235,000 students estimated to be in private schools. This means an increase of almost 290,000 since 1970.

Given the startling growth of Christian segregationist academies that can be seen casually throughout the South, the project is satisfied that they account for this increase in enrollment.

Thus the study arrives at an assumption that admittedly is not provable but which the project's participants believe is accurate that some 750,000 students in the South are in the schools and receiving the kind of education to which the project devotes itself. Casual observation also suggests that the schools are consistently small, with an average of some 200 students per school; thus between three and four thousand schools may exist as essentially segregationist academies in the thirteen southern states.

3

Schools for Whites

These are schools for whites. The common thread that runs through them all, Christian, secular, or otherwise, is that they provide white ground to which blacks are admitted only on the school's terms if at all.

The question is more complicated than the simple racism that marked the 1960s but obviously race is a key ingredient in the new schools. Their growth follows school integration. In rural areas they sprang up at the first sign of integration and in cities they followed busing orders. Many had their first and only surge of growth in the year following the order.

The schools grow from white flight from integrated public schools. They prosper most in those communities which lack a nearby haven and least in the places where fleeing whites have someplace to go. The most striking growth of the new private schools in America, for example, is in Memphis, where since 1970 the total number of schools has risen from 41 to more than 125, with enrollment rising from 12,000 to more than 37,000. This obviously is related to the fact that as unincorporated communities served by county schools arise on its borders, Memphis regularly annexes them and assumes control of their schools, which brings them under the Memphis court order. The only havens within commuting distance are across state lines, in Arkansas and Mississippi, a major move for many people. In Atlanta, on the other hand, though the city schools are only 11 per cent white, the new private schools have not grown markedly. The difference seems to be that Atlanta is surrounded by other counties and jurisdictions which provide equally convenient living but are not served by Atlanta schools.

While the new schools certainly are products of white flight, it appears that they are not a cause of white flight—a most important distinction.

White flight may be a reaction to integration orders. It certainly is a reaction to what is perceived as trouble in the public schools, a perception that is very widely held among the middle class conservative people who are the chief patrons of the private schools.

The point is narrow, but it seems clear that white flight grows from a number of reasons, including long-term historic city-to-suburb trends. The effect of the new private schools is to make the move comfortable. For instance, Memphis public schools in the period noted above lost some 44,000 students, of whom 25,000 went to private schools. Where did the other 19,000 go? No one knows, though obviously some went across state lines and some dropped out of school. Were there no private schools, some of the 25,000 presumably would be back in public school—but many would have joined their fellows elsewhere.

But the private schools *were* there and thus provided a comfortable haven, which is their real function. For those who wanted to flee and could afford tuition, there was no need to move the family or to send a child to an aunt in another town when a segregationist academy awaited just down the street. Thus the new schools exacerbate the trouble in the public schools, but their involvement is after the fact.

Some schools, of course, are openly segregationist. The most blatant example is the Council schools of Mississippi, most of which are in Jackson. They are operated by the Council School Foundation, which was formed by the Citizens Council in response to the passage of the Civil Rights Act of 1964. The schools remain as hostile as ever. The 1975-1976 enrollment application, for example, opens with this statement:

"It is the belief of the Board of Directors of Council School Foundation that forced congregation of persons in social situations solely because they are of different races is a moral wrong, and it is the further belief of the Board of Directors that the proven educational results of such forced interracial congregation are disastrous for children of both the white and black races. Council School Foundation was founded upon and is operated in accordance with this fundamental ethical and educational concept. ·

"The currculum of Council School Foundation is designed solely for the educational responses of white children. It follows, therefore, that only those students who are innately capable of a satisfactory learning response, in a true peer group, to this curriculum are qualified for enrollment . . ."

In a copyrighted booklet the Foundation observed that the terms of the Civil Rights Act made it clear that public schools had been "placed under the control of the federal courts," and thus "became federal schools." In a curious additional note, it went on to suggest that it feels out of step with the mainstream, insisting that integration is "disastrous," and that this "is true, and is acknowledged by the way some people act, although for some unknown reason many avoid mentioning the subject, as if by not doing so it will go away."

The first Council school opened in September 1964, and by the next year had 110 students. A second school opened in 1967. In 1969, with a major integration order imminent in Jackson, the Council schools began to boom. By the 1971-1972 school year total enrollment in six schools was 5,300 students. Thereafter, enrollment leveled out at about 6,000 and in recent years may have declined. The schools no longer release enrollment figures to state authorities or to the public, but there have been persistent reports of shrinkage and of parents transferring children to other academies which offer a less doctrinaire political outlook.

One of the critical questions about the new schools is the extent to which they are helped by public schools and public money. In smaller communities in the 1960s they sometimes in effect replaced the public schools, so far as the white community was concerned. Entire student bodies moved from formerly all-white public schools to new private schools. They took along the trappings of the old school, its colors, its teams, mascots, symbols, its student newspaper, leaving behind the shell of the building. Often the public school board and its officials seem to view the new schools as the real schools of the community and a great deal of covert and some overt assistance was given them. Books, furniture, buses and even buildings were turned over to private schools or sold for a fraction of their value. Communities paved roads to new schools, let them use public school gyms, helped them light their playing fields. Alabama tried to make tuition grants to private schools on five occasions. Tennessee tried three times. The Supreme Court set all these plans aside, as it did Mississippi's system of giving state texts to private schools. Documents filed in that case showed that in 1970 the state had 173,424 books worth $490,239 in 107 white segregationist schools and expected to spend $200,000 a year thereafter keeping these books up to date.

Gradually, however, such practices have declined. From time to time reports of state assistance to private schools appear, but they seem of negligible importance overall. Attitudes about desegregation have evolved in the South and the idea of illegal resistance seems to have passed. The new school movement itself has grown, stabilized, solidified and become much more sophisticated. It has learned that it can survive without such help.

Upon starting, many private schools managed to buy used books and furniture that public schools had declared surplus, and it is hard to tell whether collusion was involved. Certainly the books and furniture in most of the schools are so battered that it is easy to imagine that a modern school system would replace them legitimately. A few private academies probably still are getting a little covert help from local public schools, but the problem seems relatively minor.

Similarly, there appears little support for the frequent rumors that right-wing political money is behind the new schools. Most schools have relatively little capital investment and give the impression of struggling from one tuition period to the next. The few exceptions in terms of building and equipment gave sound explanations for their funding which, among those checked, their banks supported. The idea of political money may be more wishful thinking than fact; one young pastor who had just started a school wistfully asked a member of the project if he knew where one could apply for such money.

The other great area in which government policy affects the support given the new schools is in federal tax rules. A few schools are proprietary and a very few are quite profitable, but most operate as tax exempt charitable institutions, which gives them a real advantage at public expense. The exemption lets them plow any profits back into the school, but the real importance is that donations are deductible on personal income tax returns. This is critical to those "faith pledge rallies" that so many schools hold as they get started; it is a form of public assistance in that it reduces tax income to government.

Until 1970 racial discrimination was not considered in determining a school's tax exempt status. As the result of a landmark case—*Green vs. Connally*, which held, among other things, that racial segregation was contrary to United States policy as articulated by Congress—the Internal Revenue Service issued new regulations requiring schools to demonstrate non-discriminatory policies in order to qualify for tax exemptions. It issued guidelines describing the form that demonstration was to take. In 1972, as part of its response to the court's orders in *Green*, it sent a questionnaire to all tax-exempt schools asking them for what amounted to assurances of non-discriminatory policies. Those that refused to answer or admitted discrimination or that could not establish non-discrimination had their tax exemptions suspended. Since then, the IRS says, it has judged new applications for tax exempt status against the guidelines. Other than reviewing a school's initial application, however, it makes no further check on compliance except on a random or spot-check basis, similar to random audits of individuals or businesses. The percentage of tax returns audited varies for different organiza-

15

tions; the IRS will not say what percentage of private school returns are reviewed for assurances of non-discrimination.

The IRS is more interested in collecting taxes than in enforcing social policy and it seems to have approached the issue of reviewing school exemptions with real reluctance. Since 1970, it reports, a total of 106 schools have lost their tax exemptions; about three-quarters of these cases grew directly from the survey of 1972. The IRS has no figures on how many have been refused exemptions on their initial application, but assumes there would be some in this category.

Considering that thousands of these schools have been started in direct response to integrated public schools and that the most casual acquaintance with the schools makes clear that their purpose is to serve only whites, it is surprising that only 106 have been judged discriminatory.

In November 1975, the IRS published new guidelines which are a little stricter. Schools must make a statement of non-discrimination in their charter and in their printed literature, and must advertise the statement. They must attest that they function in a non-discrimina-tory manner. This may tighten the net a little, but it seems doubtful that many more schools will lose their exemptions, however obvious their role as havens for fleeing whites.

There are a couple of reasons for this apparent discrepancy. The conclusion is inescapable that the IRS doesn't check very diligently whether its guidelines are adequate or how seriously a school tries to meet them. It audits schools on a routine basis and responds to com-plaints in the same manner. It tends to accept the schools' statements at face value and rarely moves in with field investigators. When the tax exemption is in the name of a supporting or owning church, the IRS may not even know that a school is involved and therefore has no occasion to examine its operation. The tax violations that appear to interest the IRS turn around fraud, not race.

The second point is that schools today are more willing to make a minimal effort toward a limited open admissions policy because they have found that they can do so with no real expectation of blacks enrolling. As the new school movement has become more sophisticated, many new schools have abandoned anti-black rhetoric. As middle class whites in the South have become more conscious of their image in racial matters, they have begun to say (and to believe) that they have many reasons for patronizing the schools that have little to do with race. To support this, they must be willing to accept a few blacks. This is easy enough because it is only in theory; in practice, blacks aren't interested in the schools. Why should they pay to put their children in an all-white environment for a poor education? As one civil rights advocate observed, "It's an insult to ask a black child to enroll in a school established to avoid integration after he has waited fifteen or twenty years for public schools to desegregate." It appears that black children would be uncomfortable in most of the new schools and endangered in some, but that doesn't keep the schools from advertising an open admissions policy. Parental attitudes seem to be that so long as no blacks or only a few blacks come, let the schools advertise as they like.

On a separate issue, the U.S. Supreme Court recently denied the right of two private schools in Virginia to exclude black children. The question here was not tax exemption but whether a private school may legally segregate. The argument turned on an 1866 law that guarantees all citizens "the same right in every state and territory to make and enforce contracts." Obviously the Court's decision is important on principle, but it probably won't make much practical difference. It seems very unlikely that blacks in any numbers will be interested in patronizing the new schools.

The fact that many new schools can meet the IRS guidelines readily and still maintain their original character and that only 106 exemptions have been revoked in six years points up the fact that the guidelines themselves are minimal and that enforcement probably is less than minimal. This raises the question of whether schools whose practice is so clearly contrary to the stated policy of the nation should receive public support in the form of the tax exemption. It will be tested soon in a suit which the Lawyers' Committee for Civil Rights Under Law has filed against the IRS. The Lawyers' Committee brought the action that led to the *Green* decision. The new suit urges the revocation of tax exempt status for organizations such as churches which support schools with discriminatory policies, a check the IRS doesn't make at this point. The headmaster of one such school, for example, a small and rigidly fundamentalist place supported by an equally rigid church, said, "I suppose it's just a matter of time until the IRS catches up with us, but I hope it doesn't come before the church itself has taken action on the question."

The issue, as a Committee lawyer put it, "is the right of whites to set up alternative institutions that circumvent national policy and then to get government support." The Committee will contend that any private school that is virtually all white and is near a school district that has had major desegregation orders should be presumed to be a haven; the burden, in Committee's view, should be on the school to prove that it is not a haven, is not discriminatory and therefore deserves the tax exemption.

The suit, however decided, should go a long way toward clarifying United States policy and determining just how much public assistance the new schools should be allowed.

4

The Fear That Built
the Schools

The success of the new schools is significant to the polarization of American society. The schools contradict the idea that the surface quiet of the 1970s means that the divisions of the 1960s are healing. In this sense, the new schools are a new form of action, significant in both magnitude and commitment.

The men and women who start the new schools, the parents who support them and the children who attend them, seem to share a similar and pessimistic view of society. Essentially, they complain of change. They mirror the themes of the textbook controversy at Kanawha County, West Virginia. Life is moving ever faster and they don't like its direction. With uniformity that finally becomes startling, they link into one disconcerting, unsavory whole the things they find disturbing—the end of the old-fashioned patriotism, the new view of America's role in the world, the changing attitude toward authority and leaders, shrinking church attendance, rising divorce rates, acceptance of pre-marital sex, dirty movies, public nudity, foul language, the loosening of constraint and custom, abortion, crime, drugs, erosion of the work ethic, textbooks that question old values and old heroes and the countless other manifestations of a new view of themselves that many Americans now are entertaining. We have become soft, they say, permissive, afraid of divisive elements in our society. We have lost the concept of discipline as a virtue. The list comes as a litany of dismay: they believe they see a disintegrating society. They seem to feel threatened when the law protects the minority from the majority. They are, after all, the majority—white, affluent, successful, middle class, middle American. As the powerless—women, minorities, employees, even students—assert rights under law, this majority seems to see itself as newly powerless, as severed from a society it cannot control but cannot accept.

It is not news that people feel alienated and powerless, and believe that their institutions have abandoned them and even turned on them. But the difference here is that the people who start and support the new schools are taking action in a specific way. They are taxing themselves heavily to open alternative schools, ones that stress their values, their attitudes, their principles of morality and right. It is no accident that the schools oppose the thrust of the society as a whole. That is their purpose.

As one talks to proprietors and patrons of the new schools, there seems much more than simple protest and more than simple racism in their attitudes. Rather they suggest a sense of mission comparable to other social movements in which people are determined to take control of their lives and of the institutions that affect their lives. Just as the public schools have been chosen as a place to try to correct an overall injustice in American society, so these people are using their schools to try to correct what they perceive as dangerous and grievously wrong turns the society has taken. In creating enclaves in which their children's lives can go on seemingly unchanged, they are evidencing an attitude that clearly transcends education as such and may represent a measurable expansion of the alienation of the last decade.

At the same time, however, they are responding to their perception of public schools as exemplifying the trends they deplore in society. It is not our purpose to explore the manifold problems of public schools in a changing society except as they relate to the willingness of the patrons of the new schools to meet costs that amount to double and triple what they already are paying in school taxes. In brief, their view of public schools is that they are horrid and dangerous places. They believe schools are full of drugs, sexual license and fighting; that white teachers are intimidated by black students, and black teachers can't handle students of either race; that classrooms are chaotic, discipline has vanished and learning has stopped. They insist that this describes the experience of their own children in public schools (though the project found no one whose child actually had been hurt).

The view seems exaggerated, but two broad points deserve attention. First, public schools do reflect the turmoil of a changing society. As society questions its values, schools reflect those questions; as style, morality and outlook change in the society, so they change in the schools. A series of court decisions supporting the right of students—and, for that matter, of teachers—to due process has changed the old dictatorial manner that once ruled schools. It is useful to remember that the public schools which the parents and ad-ministrators of the new schools recall so fondly from their own youth were operating at a time when neither schools nor society were questioning the future.

Second, integration has brought into the mainstream of southern schools children from disproportionately disadvantaged socio-economic background—another cruel legacy of American racism. When black youngsters were segregated, the fact that some had learning disadvantages—which now is seen largely as a function of socio-economic class—was ignored. In one of its more specific ad-vantages, integration forced public schools to begin to deal realistically with those disadvantaged youngsters. It also changed the nature of the clients in individual schools, which until then had been essentially homogenous and run with little regard for the rights of students. In adjusting to different kinds of students and teachers and different social realities, the schools naturally are not the same middle class segregated enclaves which patrons of the new schools remember from their own youth.

The view these patrons hold of society and their willingness to tax themselves to support alternative schools are affected by the nature of evangelical Protestantism, which lies directly behind Christian schools and indirectly behind secular schools. It is the largest and fastest growing stream in Protestantism and may have forty million members in America. As other churches shrink, various evangelical denominations are booming. This is especially important in the South, where evangelical religion has long held sway. Evangelical Protestantism is not synonymous with the new schools, of course; the new schools seem to spring from its right wing and many moderate Baptists, for example, are disturbed by the schools' growth and the consequent erosion of support for the public schools.

The attitudes of fundamentalism touch the new schools in various ways, especially in curriculum and choice of teachers, and are best examined under those headings. A few general points which bear on the schools as a whole might be noted here. One is that evangelical faiths are based on a strict and literal reading of the Bible which is regarded as a once-and-forever delivered corpus of truth from outside history inserted into history through revelation. Such Christians tend to reject what often is called the modern temper, the new science and thought, when it conflicts with their interpretation of the revealed truth of God, which it often seems to do. Presumably this is in part a problem of interpreting an ancient document in modern light, but it certainly has the effect of making many of the thrusts of modern education seem dubious to fundamental Christians. And since they operate not from a flexible, ever-changing perception of the world around them but from an immutable truth revealed trans-historically by God, naturally they pursue their way with great confidence.

Another important point is that the evangelical act itself may be seen as the essential act of the evangelical church, as the act of eucharist is the essential act of certain other branches of the Christian church. The words evangelical and angel flow from the same source, implying "messenger bearing good news," and the evangelical Christian is expected to be a salesman for his point-of-view, "to go to the ends of the earth and preach the gospel to every creature." Thus the evangelical church puts its emphasis not on ritual but on the act of preaching itself, which means that the preeminent preacher validates himself in the very deepest sense by his capacity in the pulpit where his pronouncements on the state of society and its relationship to God's teaching have great force. Since aggressive preaching of the gospel and carrying of God's word is basic, the idea of starting schools which are infused with it follows naturally in a time when believers find that public schools are moving away from it. Proselytizing, exhorting the young student to come forward and be saved by accepting Christ and washing away his sins, also is basic to the purpose of the evangelical church. Many pastors who also run new schools describe with enthusiasm the number of conversions their school has produced; that, as one put it in echo of many, "is really what it's all about," and from the viewpoint of evangelical faith, of course, they are correct.

Perhaps in part because each man is expected to make his own interpretation of the Bible, great schisms run through the evangelical church. There is a feeling among many new school people, for example, that Billy Graham is dangerously far to the left if not already a captive of worldly, modernist forces. This decrying of liberalism within fundamentalism often becomes entwined with a deep distaste for political liberalism as well. This grows in part from the fact that political and church liberalism both tend to emphasize the value of the individual human and thus to equate goodness with kindness to one's fellow men. In the fundamentalist faith, one's salvation depends on faith in God, not on one's decency to one's fellows. Emphasis on the latter, it is suggested, detracts from the former. Yet modern American society—and modern education—equate what is good and desirable with what benefits other people. From the fundamentalist viewpoint, the effect of the welfare state is to expand a man-to-man relationship and detract from a man-to-God relationship. This same attitude can be tracked through most aspects of modern social institutions; the strictest fundamentalist Christian tends to find most of modern society irrelevant if not actually inconsistent with the strictures of his faith.

Taken all together, then, it is not surprising that fundamentalists find themselves dissatisfied with the modern society and its schools, and are willing to open alternative schools that reflect their viewpoints more clearly.

5

The Starting Process

As this acute view of American society as a failed institution has gradually superseded mere resistance to integration, the new school movement has shifted more and more from the secular academy to the Christian academy. The relationship of the movement to integration orders remains clear, however. Some new schoolmen admit frankly that they wouldn't have started—or couldn't have—without the impetus of an integration order. "I am revolting against busing," one parent said, explaining everything in five words. More commonly, schoolmen say they did not begin as havens but that they have been helped by the situation. "We'd have begun anyway," one who spoke for many said, "but the busing order gave us five to ten years of growth compressed into one year."

Much of the integration since *Swann* has been in urban areas, where it is much more difficult than in a rural situation to create community-wide organizations. The experience in Greene County, Alabama, and that of the Citizens Against Busing schools in Memphis make useful comparison. When an integration order was handed down in rural Sumter County, where some 80 per cent of the people are black, the white students moved *en masse* to Sumter Academy. In neighboring Greene County, the white students trooped to Warrior Academy, another newly opened school. Sumter Academy opened in 1970 with 400 students and has remained remarkably stable; in 1975, it had 569 students. A recent count showed 37 white students in public school in Greene County: in Sumter County, the count of white students has risen from a low of six to 135.

The Citizens Against Busing schools in Memphis, on the other hand, organized in a flash but encountered immediate difficulty. Within a couple of weeks after the busing order was handed down there, in January 1973, this community-wide group had opened 26 schools with more than 5,000 students. By the following fall, however, with their organization cracking apart, they were down to four schools with 600 students, and at the end of that semester they were gone. Their students had not gone back to public school—they had shifted to new church schools.

Such a community-wide organization is unstable almost by definition in a large community. A local fundamentalist church, on the other hand, is both homogenous and highly stable. It is the only organization which its members control at a time when they feel government institutions are out of control. It is often the only structure they trust and certainly the one in which they feel most comfortable, since much of their social as well as their spiritual life revolves around it.

Startling numbers of the patrons of the new schools will say quite independently of each other that public school problems really began when the Supreme Court outlawed prayer and Bible reading there. Such is the nature of fundamentalism that these people usually mention school devotions and pledges of allegiance to the flag in the same breath and see them as inseparable. Turning to their church from such viewpoint thus is entirely natural; indeed, their church provides their only antidote for society as they view it.

Often their church is nearby and certainly it is in a neighborhood like theirs if not in their neighborhood. This appeals to the widely held if probably false issue of the sanctity of neighborhood schools. (The issue probably is false because the whole story of improving public schools through consolidation runs against the neighborhood concept and because people are perfectly willing to bus their children for miles to Christian schools, but it nevertheless is an article of faith with patrons of the new schools.)

Since fundamentalist churches are Bible-based, they put heavy emphasis on Sunday School for people of all ages, which means that most such churches have school rooms which lie idle for most of the week. Indeed, most Protestant churches have religious education facilities that are vacant for most of the week. In the South this has provided an immediate physical base for an alternative school system. Even the Citizens Against Busing schools, described above, though they were secular in operation, were actually located in churches.

In addition to physical school rooms, the church offers a financial structure that can support a school. It offers a framework that its people can support emotionally; because they trust their minister, who can support his moral views with a deeper reading of the Bible than they can manage, they take comfort in his assurance that they are moving in the right direction. And the church structure also allows them to support schools with tax-deductible gifts.

The nature of the usual fundamentalist church is more geared toward such action than away from it. A pastor who is anxious to go forward with a school—and many see it as a means of building a bigger church—can usually sway his congregation to follow him. On the other hand, some pastors who have tried to resist the new schools have literally been turned around by unanimous congregations. The pastor has considerable power, but since these churches are totally independent, he has no hierarchy to turn to for assistance when his congregation wants to move in a certain direction. If his people are determined, he leads them where they want to go lest he be left out completely.

Many new schools are started as an emotional reaction to an integration order. Interviews with many parents and schoolmen suggest that they already were frightened; in discussing the order, surprising numbers use the analogy of the straw and the camel's back.

This element of hysteria accounts for the fact that many schools start suddenly and achieve the bulk of their growth immediately. A few continue to grow, but most settle down to a struggle of trying to hold their own.

In that initial period, however, the new schools become a movement, a form of continuing the battle against the order. The Citizens Against Busing schools were supported by huge public rallies at which buckets were passed for collections. People made and sold candy door-to-door to raise money, and established school fairs and other fund-raising events. Since the movement had a religious fervor, it is not surprising that it soon transferred itself directly into churches.

In Louisville, Kentucky, after a busing order in the fall of 1975 produced considerable public reaction, a group of evangelical church ministers held a meeting to talk about starting a school. Several expressed reluctance to shoulder the responsibility until Don Grice, pastor of the Louisville Baptist Tabernacle, offered his building. Grice had started the church four years earlier—in a building taken over from a bankrupt pentecostal church—and despite its ambitious title it was still small. He had built it from scratch to about 300 members. Filled with the confidence he says he draws from prayer, Grice turned an already scheduled "God and Country Rally" on October 12 into a referendum on the school proposal and got unanimous approval from the 400 who attended. The next morning he decided to go ahead and exactly two weeks later, October 27, 1975, Shively Christian School opened with 105 students.

Kentucky codes governing schools are a little stricter than in some states (some have no school codes beyond fire and sanitation matters), and Grice set about bringing his school into physical compliance with state law. Using much donated labor, he ripped out the walls of the small Sunday School rooms on the second floor and converted them to regular classrooms. He installed new lights, enlarged the bathrooms, put in an improved furnace and opened with some $50,000 invested by his own and other churches.

Meanwhile he had found a former public school teacher who had served as principal of another fundamentalist church school—a woman of considerable competence—to head the academic side of the new school. She engaged teachers, purchased used textbooks, established curriculum and teaching patterns and opened for business. Within a few weeks, as word of the school spread, its enrollment was bumping the limit of 200 beyond which it could not go without opening a new building.

Grice had planned to have only a grade school, but he encountered such parental pressure that he ended in accepting 65 students of high school age. They attended classes in the pews of the church sanctuary which were divided into four rooms by partitions that were taken down for Sunday services. Grice ordered "desks" which could be clipped onto the back of the next pew and high school went forward.

It was just the beginning—but in fact, it was quite a typical beginning.

Most of the schools start in a hurry. Most begin with inadequate plans which they make little attempt to improve beyond minimum codes. Most start with what often is called a "faith rally" at which members pledge backing. "When a group of middle class people get together and pledge," one experienced minister said, "it is not hard to raise the money. Many of these people command considerable property and wealth and just about all of them are able to pledge up to, oh, say $1,500, and meet it out of future earnings." He made it clear these are people uniformly distressed not only with current integration orders but with the state of society and the public schools, and for whom the idea of a church school is not entirely new.

Typically the new schools' patrons include a high proportion of people in the building trades who are willing to donate huge amounts of labor, often working through weekends and late at night under floodlights. The ramrod of one such school in Charlotte was himself an electrical contractor. He not only wired the entire school by himself but rallied business associates who poured in free labor plus equipment and supplies purchased at bare cost.

The capacity of a typical segregationist academy to solidify is seen in the experience of Elliston Baptist Academy in Memphis, where the new schools are most of all successful. Elliston Baptist Church is in a working section of the city. Its pastor is Brother Floyd

Simmons, a strong, confident man who looks and sounds rather like a younger John Wayne.

"Integration wasn't it," he said. "We've been integrating in Memphis for years. Our kids were the first to be bused, that's what it was about. I would never have dreamed of starting a school, hadn't it been for busing. Well, our people were concerned and we prayed about it. Now I've been in the ministry for 25 years and this was the only time the Lord ever got me up in the night. And He said, 'Get the Book, I want to show you what to do.' I opened the Book and I found the answer. Oh, the thing was so clear. The first time it fell open in the New Testament, the second time in the Old. This was a Tuesday night and the following night I made a report to the church and we decided to start. We had six months to get ready."

The most experienced teacher Simmons drew into the new school had five years in public school and she took over developing the curriculum. They gave church families first opportunity to enroll and then opened to the public. The school had 320 students in the first semester and 550 the next. Simmons borrowed $350,000 from a bank and—using free labor from the church—built a gym with classrooms that later was appraised at $750,000. After the second year he borrowed another $200,000 and put up another building on donated property across the street. Enrollment in ten grades, with the eleventh and twelfth added year by year, shot up to 1,800, then leveled off at about 1,550.

Simmons needed an administrator and brought in a big, cheerful man named Oscar Ammer, who had been an assistant principal in a public school. Ammer had never considered such a move until he suddenly was converted and joined Simmons' church. He and Simmons prayed over the headmastership and Ammer agreed to take it. Ammer was in perfect agreement with Simmons' view that the real problem with youngsters today is their failure to cling to the faith, a quality exacerbated by their public school experience.

"I found that 25 to 40 per cent of the kids were agnostics," Simmons said. "Part of the school's mission is to bring them to the faith. At least a thousand kids in the last three years have made public decisions for Christ in the school, and that's what it's all about."

Simmons feels that he started on faith and survives on faith. "I had an accountant who went haywire," he said. "He looked at the figures and he could project that we would be broke by sometime last year. You see, if you take faith out of a program, you have nothing left. If we had not started without money, we wouldn't have started. Of course, if I had known then that I would face a $56,000 monthly payroll, maybe I wouldn't have started the school."

Simmons regards the school as a service to the church and the community. The children of members who tithe are admitted without further charge, and children from the community are rarely turned away for lack of funds. "We're not in the collecting business," Simmons said. "Many of them, the outside families, haven't paid, and we just write it off as 'no charge.' Anyway, we're not in the red. We meet our payrolls and pay our bills."

The extent of the individual success of a new school does depend on where it is located, and many small schools do limp along in constant financial trouble that makes them very vulnerable to parental pressure. But the movement itself appears to be fundamentally viable and segregationist academies are likely to be a permanent part of the education picture in the South. The schools tend to institutionalize as they grow and survive the first few troublesome years. They establish themselves firmly with a permanent teacher corps, an established if still narrow curriculum, athletic teams that usually play in Christian leagues, school papers, drama clubs, debate teams, and other activities. An Atlanta school founded in 1958, for example, has one teacher with 14 years service and a number with more than 10 years. It is proud of its tradition; already earlier graduating classes return to visit.

In Charlotte in 1962, Brother W. Jack Hudson, who had been an auto racer and garage owner before the ministry called, opened a school with 44 students at his Northside Baptist Church. His church has grown from 29 members less than twenty years ago to a membership of 5,000, and his school (admittedly with some help from *Swann*) has grown to more than 850 students with a teaching staff of 45 in a handsome building which adjoins Northside's new church building.

At their most successful the new schools expand into systems, achieving economy of scale, expansion of program and a great deal of flexibility. This institutionalization process is important because it implies a certification of the new movement and assures its permanence. This process is further along in Memphis, where the schools are atypically expanded because of special circumstances, but the effect is one of fundamental permanence reaching far beyond the city. There are many single schools there, of course, but the key difference in the Memphis model is the presence of *systems* of new schools.

Ten churches in Memphis joined to form the Southern Baptist Educational Center which operates from a handsome new $2 million building on a 36-acre campus and has 1,270 students.

Thirteen churches joined on Memphis' north side to form Frayser Baptist Schools, which have five grade schools in various churches feeding a single high school which is being constructed on a 34-acre plot. It now has 760 students and points toward 1,200.

Harding Academy, the old Church of Christ school which has chosen to limit its enrollment to 3,000, now operates ten grade schools which channel graduates to a high school. Among other things, it prepares a hot lunch daily in a central kitchen and delivers it to each school by truck.

Evangelical Christian School has operated for more than a decade as a super-fundamentalist enclave for people who long have been out of sympathy with public schools. Since the surge of growth in Memphis, its enrollment has risen to almost a thousand students in four elementaries and a new high school in a handsome modernistic building.

But the most extraordinary, among the biggest and certainly among the best of the new schools anywhere is the Briarcrest Baptist School System, which operates thirteen elementaries and a high school. The elementaries can handle 2,600 students, the high school 1,600. Enrollment in the fall of 1975 was about 90 per cent of capacity—2,359 in the elementaries, 1,431 in the high school. This is the system to which George Barton and his wife pay some twelve per cent of their salaries earned in the Firestone tire plant in Memphis and count themselves lucky that their three children are so well taught.

The Briarcrest story is a good place to observe this institution- alizing trend. The story begins with the eruption of the Citizens Against Busing schools after the January 1973 court order in Memphis. "Memphis doesn't know how to react to things," said Mrs. Ruth Saed, an initial CAB organizer, "and if we hadn't provided an alternative, there'd have been violence for sure."

It is intriguing that the vigorous anti-violence campaign waged by the Memphis Chamber of Commerce usually is given credit for the fact that no heads were broken—credit that Mrs. Saed takes for her schools, which grew out of excited mass rallies. "We had to do something," she said, "to keep people from going crazy."

Within two weeks, CAB's 26 schools were open with a semblance of instruction for their 5,000 youngsters. They hired teachers overnight and bought desks at one dollar apiece and were given surplus textbooks at the public school surplus warehouse. When this appeared in the press, the Board of Education closed its warehouse.

Meanwhile, two men were playing different but parallel roles in the institutionalization process that was beginning with these make- shift schools. One was Bob Agee, then pastor of Ardmore Baptist Church, and the other was Wayne Allen, pastor of East Park Baptist Church and founder of Briarcrest. Agee is a slender, soft-spoken, moderate, intelligent man who since has returned to the academic world where he probably is more comfortable. Allen is 36 years old, a huge man who weighs 325 pounds and towers over his parishioners, a thunderous evangelical preacher radiating piety and optimism who hurls his people along on the force of his voice.

Many Memphis ministers resisted the CAB organizers. Agee turned them down despite pressure from his church. He saw them as rabble rousers, and he believed in public education. He was at the public high school almost daily, ameliorating conflicts among students. Allen also turned down the CAB schools—he had his own plans.

P.O. Davidson, pastor of a church near Agee's, tried to refuse CAB, but his congregation turned him around with a unanimous vote. He saw the CAB school that began in his buildings as disastrous, drawing rude, violent people who were destructive and out of control. They wrecked his building and he threw them out after a semester.

But Carl Quattlebaum at Cottonwood Heights Baptist Church thought the CAB school in his building was satisfactory. Nevertheless, he built a building to state construction standards and opened his own school after the first semester.

And indeed, by the fall of 1973, CAB schools had declined from 26 to 4 locations with 600 students and in another semester CAB was out of business.

But it had had its effect. Agee, for example, could no longer resist the pressure in his church. Now he saw private schools as inevitable and decided that at least he could take them out of the hands of the rabble rousers. With P.O. Davidson and eleven other pastors, he formed the Frayser system.

By the fall of 1973, Brother Allen was in the business he says he always had planned. His call to the ministry came when he was thirteen and he has been preaching ever since. The public high school he was attending refused to let him preach in its halls, so he hired an old van, parked it in front of the school and held services every morning. And right there, he says, he began to dream of a Christian school.

When he came to East Park five years ago, it was a failing church. By 1973 he had tripled its membership and he moved naturally into the opportunity provided by the busing crisis. Allen is a classic entrepreneurial preacher. He believes in what he calls the superchurch concept which provides total activity and entertainment for its people in an evangelical setting. He has missions to local jails and to Africa, where he flies to save souls. When he was asked about reaching out to Memphis blacks, his answer outlined his theology: "No need to—they already know Jesus." But race isn't a specific issue with him. His schools have a stated open admission policy. A young black woman joined his church recently.

Allen put together a chain of elementary schools in neighborhood churches and planned a high school. His congregation, already overflowing its quarters, had decided it needed a new building and was seeking suitable ground. He found just what he needed, 14.5 acres near a beltway, a location that could draw people from all over Memphis. He held a prayer session, got unanimous approval and bid $30,000 an acre, plus $500. Another group wanted to put a synagogue there. It bid $30,000 plus $100. Allen sees this as a direct intervention of God. One of his parishioners, Mrs. Vayden Waddy, remembers that on their way to the bid opening, her husband was fretting anxiously. "I told him, 'What's the matter with you, Waddy? God doesn't want Judaism to expand—he wants Christianity to expand. What are you worrying about?' "

In a rather startling departure—which itself might be described as an act of faith—they decided to erect a building which would serve as both high school and church. They asked an architect for a school with a 2,000-seat auditorium that would have pews instead of theater seats. The classrooms in simple reversal of the usual would serve as Sunday School rooms. The resulting building is handsome and certainly adequate. The auditorium, rich in burnished orange and polished wood, works well on Sundays; on weekdays a big bronze dove hanging on the wall hides the baptistry. The building's cafeteria serves 750 at once, its gym seats 1,000 with room for two basketball games at once, its classrooms are large, well lighted, air conditioned and carpeted, and its labs appear well appointed. Its athletic teams challenge public schools. Its textbooks are state approved, its library is adequate, its teachers are state certified with degrees in their teaching areas, the school is state approved and is going through the final steps for accreditation by the Southern Association. Its principal, Joseph Clayton, had an outstanding reputation in Memphis public schools, where his departure still is lamented.

The total cost crept from an original $4 million to $6.5 million. "When you've bit down on four million," said Therrell Pressgrove, a deacon, "six million doesn't bother you too much." They held a "faith pledge picnic," at which 400 church members pledged about $1 million. They still owe about $4 million and Neil Thompson, a deacon and branch bank manager, believes they'll have no trouble meeting it. He calculates the school's income at $3,100,000 a year, after all, and church membership is now up to 1,500.

Thus Allen started a system, with considerable efficiency of scale. Carl Quattlebaum, after a year of operating a school of his own, yielded to economics and joined Briarcrest. It was just a matter of scale, he said, unconsciously adopting the argument for public schools, because a single school can't offer much. The Briarcrest system is different from others in Memphis because it is owned and operated entirely by East Park Baptist Church. East Park pays those churches where its elementary schools are lodged just enough rent to cover utilities and custodial care, thus limiting capital investment to the high school.

The decision to combine church with a big school building of excellent quality is the real mark of institutionalization, for it leaves its owners no choice but to continue. Briarcrest and the other systems in Memphis are here to stay. There is too much money, too much effort, too much conviction invested to believe the schools will fade away. Other schools in other places may find circumstances less favorable and the struggle more difficult—but the lesson of institutionalization in Memphis is that the concept of the new schools is viable and permanent.

6

The Atmosphere
in the Schools

The philosophic nature of the new schools is dominated by religion. This is most of all true, of course, in the Christian schools, but even in the secular schools, a strong religious orientation underlies the schools' basic purposes and attitudes. New school people assert that public school problems began with—and perhaps were the result of—the ban on prayer which now is more than a decade old.

Almost invariably the new schools open classes with prayer and often this is expanded into a considerable devotional exercise, with readings from the Bible. In schools affluent enough to afford the equipment, this frequently is given by an older student over the school loudspeaker.

Hand-in-hand with the opening prayer is the pledge of allegiance to the United States flag. Patriotism seems to intertwine with religion in the minds of most patrons of the new schools; much of their distaste for modern society arises from what they see as a slackening in the love of country and a new tendency to belittle patriotism, the flag and the nation's military adventures. The Council schools, for example, list themselves as nonsectarian and nonpartisan, but add that the system "inculcates reverence and loyalty through devotional and patriotic exercises."

The Christian schools require Bible study as part of their regular curriculum. They also have a daily chapel with one or two sessions each week amounting to full-fledged church services, often with a thunderous sermon emphasizing the fundamentalist view of man's nature as depraved and inherently sinful, to be rescued only by acceptance of the Savior. Secular schools usually invite a minister in at least once a week; Christian schools count on a sermon from the host church pastor and from a visitor. Other services consist of Bible readings, prayer, music, visiting evangelists and sermons preached by senior students.

It is a rare Christian school that gives a student much latitude in attending services and taking part in prayer. Some schools demand that parents sign waivers that permit their children to take part in all religious activities. This attitude flows from the fact that the Christian schoolman feels that religious training is the basic reason for the school's existence.

"The Christian part of school is the most important," said Oscar Ammer. "Education itself is secondary." Parents of children in Briarcrest approvingly quoted the principal there as saying, when he found a devotional running far overtime, "Keep right on—what you're doing here is more important than anything you could be learning in the classroom."

In one of the schools he studied, University of Alabama Professor Robert E. Bills encountered a woman busily restocking an impressive array of food vending machines which surprising numbers of students used as soon as school opened. She explained to Bills, "It's a matter of values. If you want your child to have a good Christian education such as they get here, both parents have to work. You have to decide if you want your child to have a good breakfast or a good Christian education."

Naturally in such an atmosphere there is a great deal of proselytizing. A few schools try to avoid undue religious pressure on students and many assert that their Bible courses are not oriented to the doctrine of the sponsoring church (evangelical churches often have narrow and quite specific interpretations of the Bible, which makes the point important). But most Christian schools make it evident to the children in their charge that fundamentalist Christian faith is the only way and that the torment of eternal hellfire awaits those depraved sinners who do not choose the route to salvation. Evangelical sermons traditionally end in the invitation to come forward to the altar and accept Jesus Christ as one's personal savior, and this invitation is a regular feature of chapel services from the smallest to the largest schools. "More than 250 kids made personal decisions for Christ in our first two years, and this is our first goal," one schoolman said. The more than 1,000 decisions made at Elliston Baptist Academy were a function of the school's size rather than unusual in intent. Ministers from less fervent denominations sometimes condemn this practice. "It seems to me that when you take an impressionable six-year-old and give him a fiery sermon, you're really frightening him into the faith, and that's not a sound basis," said a Methodist minister. But evangelical schoolmen, some of whom say they do try to insulate the youngest of their charges from such persuasion, tend to scoff at the general idea. "It's quite the other way around," one said. "I would be derelict if I did not offer them their chance to be saved."

Almost without exception, Christian schools expect their teachers to be "born-again-Christians" and to inject a Biblical application into whatever subject they are teaching. We will examine this in detail under the heading of curriculum; here it is sufficient to note that history, literature, even such matters as spelling and arithmetic, are examined from a Bible-based moral posture, while science twists and turns to account for the strictures imposed by a Bible orientation. The most significant single point, of course, is the matter of evolution; in every Christian school the study touched, evolution was taught as a godless theory running directly contrary to the Bible's truth. The secular schools encountered seemed to stay as far from such sensitive questions as possible.

Parents readily accept these educational limitations for their children, and there is every reason to think that they find their own views reflected in the church and the school. Many parents belong to evangelical churches and often to the church supporting their school. One of the more radical schools insists that at least one of the parents be able to sign a profession of fundamentalist faith. So common is this relationship that the principal of a Christian school in Atlanta appeared as a major exception when he said that many parents of children in his school answered no when asked if they were part of a church. Many Christian schools see the school as a logical extension of the host church. Most give preference to children of member families, and some charge no tuition to member families who tithe. The Briarcrest system in Memphis opens registration early for members of the churches in which its elementary schools are located; the public can apply only when the host churches are satisfied.

This certainly contributes to the homogenous quality that marks these schools. Students, parents, teachers, principals, pastors all seem strikingly alike—even, it sometimes seems in the halls of the schools, in appearance. The diversity of American life here has been excluded and very high percentages would qualify as white Anglo-Saxon Protestants from middle class backgrounds. Most of the students come from unbroken homes and live in houses that stand half-paid-for in undistinguishable suburbs with a second car or a pickup outside or a small boat in the yard. Many of these families have moved from relative poverty to relative comfort by very hard work and are not yet secure in their standing. They tend to relate to monetary success, to be impatient of those less successful and to see change as a threat. Few of the new school patrons are rich; some are still quite poor and the tuition represents a sacrifice.

The children from such homes tend to be similar. Their financial support, their expectations, their opportunities are similar. Their attitude toward race, conditioned by their flight from public schools, is similar (and usually negative). Most of them belong to or are familiar with a fundamentalist church. Most of their parents share an essentially old-fashioned view of American society (which is not to say a wrong view, but rather one untouched by the doubt that the events of the last decade have imposed on many Americans). The students in the new schools seem to accept their parents' assumptions about society and the nature of life with surprising fidelity, and the school is designed to enhance and fortify these assumptions.

Wherever the rebels go, they don't go to these schools.

To the outside observer the schools, therefore, seem isolated, severed from the society in which a school ostensibly trains its students to live. Teachers seem comfortable in a situation that ignores the world; among students something like elitism seems to arise with its suggestion that they hardly need concern themselves with the world.

Thus at a time when turmoil is everywhere, the new schools appear as little islands of comfort. Part of this grows from the undeviating support the schools offer the status quo. Conversations with the new schoolmen give a clear sense of an attempt to recreate the 1950s as an ideal; another way to say this, of course, is that the new schools remind parents of the schools they knew as youngsters. For, as the schools did then, these schools deal with certainties.

The parents of these youngsters obviously find this reassuring and so, apparently, do the youngsters. One of the proudest points cited by schoolmen on behalf of their schools is the spirit they develop among students. Attendance at athletic events, now often failing in public schools, is overflowing and students wear the colors and shout the loyalty of old. Indeed, as an old public schoolman now in private education put it, "This is just the kind of school I was running twenty years ago, only then it was public. Same spirit, same dedication to learning—this is a *real* school."

An interesting if incidental aspect is that new school people subscribe to the theory of the neighborhood school, bemoan its passing and insist that their own schools fill that function. In fact, the only resemblance between the new schools and old public schools anchored to neighborhoods is that the new schools are located in suburbs. Otherwise, they are the opposite of neighborhood schools. Their clientele comes for miles, often in buses, and no neighborhood could produce the homogeneity of these schools.

The schools see hair styles and dress as expressions of student rejection of old values, and enforce dress and hair codes that range from modest at more open schools like Briarcrest to rigid at smaller and more fundamentalist-oriented schools. The most moderate school expects boys' hair to be off collars, and the stricter the school the shorter the hair. Strict schools demand that girls wear dresses and boys wear dress pants. Jeans may be convenient and durable, but many schools see them in terms of rebellion and ban them. All schools watch sharply lest girls wear clothes that may enflame boys.

The schools pride themselves on the absence of drugs, and publish strictures against the use of tobacco or alcohol. Many have closed campuses which students are not supposed to leave at noon or any other time without special permission. Some schools forbid talking in the halls and expect students to march from class to class in silence. At a rigidly fundamentalist school in Louisville, the Society's investigators found it positively eerie to be in a hall filled with children marching in silence except for the warning hisses of accompanying teachers.

All the schools emphasize discipline, though actual discipline problems seem minor in the new schools. A homogenous student body operating from the same assumptions and expectations probably produces a self-regulating pressure and makes irregular behavior less likely.

Parents, students and school people uniformly denounced what they describe as a lack of discipline in public schools, by which they mean order, enforced study, an atmosphere for learning from books. "You have to have control in order to teach," said the headmaster of a small secular school in Charlotte, "and without it you can just forget learning. In too many schools today you have to maintain constant watch, you have to check the restrooms all the time, you have to function as a policeman. That is what our parents are trying to get away from. Here—why, we don't even have locks on our lockers. There's never any theft. That's the difference in private schools."

Another difference in private schools is that, as one headmaster put it, "We don't tolerate chronic problem students and we let the parents know that at the start. We will expel the student and not refund the tuition payment. We don't have to permit disruption and we won't." To the extent that this is true—and as Professor Bills found, it may not be as clearcut as headmasters like to make it sound—it means that one reason the school is tranquil is that it can dispose of problem students. This is not a luxury permitted public schools, which must take some responsibility for every child.

Even though financial pressures probably make them more lenient than they claim, most private schools insist they do expel troublesome students and that parents understand and agree to this in advance. Most schools also use corporal punishment, again with advance parental agreement. The common instrument is a large flat wooden paddle which the principal wields, prudently calling in witnesses.

The concept of student rights has not reached these schools. Discipline begins with the teacher and when matters go beyond the classroom level, the student is dispatched to the principal as in days of old. Briarcrest uses a buck slip which the student carries to the principal. It has a number of dispositions of the case, ranging from a lecture to a paddling to being expelled. The one disposition it does not offer is the possibility that the student was right and the teacher wrong. "Oh, you never admit the teacher is wrong," said Joe Clayton, principal of Briarcrest. "Maybe you think so, and maybe you have a little talk with the teacher afterward, and maybe you finally fire the teacher if the problem is prolonged, but you never admit that to the student. That's the death of discipline."

As we have said, these are not schools for rebels, and genuine rebels certainly would be ejected. Professor Bills, whose study of student reaction to the schools is included as Part II of this book, thinks the students accept an authoritarian manner partly because they come from homes run in an authoritarian fashion and see the school as a logical and coherent extension of that atmosphere.

But there is another aspect of the schools that may lead to a countervailing sloppiness. They are totally dependent on parental support, and only the strongest are willing to demand an order of discipline that might offend a paying parent. So it would be consistent to eject summarily a student in open rebellion who would upset parents en masse while bending backward to avoid disciplining another student whose parents might be offended and withdraw child and tuition. Even with the successes of the new school movement, many individual schools still live from tuition period to tuition period, struggling to keep their heads above financial waters. Following is one churchman's description of the weight under which private schools have lived, and things today are not always so much better as to change the equation radically: "One problem of church-related schools has always been that in desperation for students to pay the bills, students were admitted with poor academic and poor conduct records and then other people would pull out their children and academic standards would be down and conduct poorer. And what happened was that anyone with a child who stole a car or got pregnant—well, send 'em to a Christian school, and see if they can't instill some decent behavior . . . "

Today's reasons are different, but the financial pressures probably are just as great for some schools. This may explain the fact that although most schools visited by the Society's investigators were quiet, orderly places, Professor Bills, who dealt most directly with students, emerged with a different view of discipline. Reluctance to impose strict discipline in day-to-day affairs may have been responsible for the slackness in operations which Bills here describes:

> "In some of the private schools there is a fear of reprimanding children because of parents' reactions and possible loss of tuition. Children often are present in the halls of some of the schools and it is difficult to determine in some schools when the day begins and ends. In one school it took 20 minutes to settle down to the task of taking the tests, in another the time was 45 minutes, and in some, children were in the corridors throughout the testing periods." (See page 102)

***

> "School starts gradually. The headmaster was to arrive at 7:30 to open the building to the examiners. He appeared at 7:50—school supposedly began at 8:00. Teachers continued to arrive and two of them appeared at 8:10. Children dragged in until 8:30.
> "At 8:45 grade 8 sent for six pencils. They had not started testing at that time. The reason was discovered later. The children were selling magazine subscriptions for the parent-teacher organization to help finance the school. The quota for each grade was $300. Grade three had raised $52 and was in difficulty. The parents say that they bought

the magazines last year and do not want them now. There were definite signs of pressure. The specific purpose of this project was to purchase lockers—there are none in the school.

"It was learned that at 8:30 the headmaster had made an announcement on the intercom (the library speaker was shut off) asking the salesmen to return to the rooms so that the testing could begin." (see page 105) *

Not incidentally, in terms of intelligence and learning capacity, Bill's tests show that youngsters in private schools are about the same as those in public schools. This leads to some unhappy parents who assume their child's failure in public schools is the fault of the schools and are dismayed to find the failure continues in the new and supposedly better private school. This is one reason, as this report will explore in more detail later, that private schools tend to emphasize the kind of rote training that produces good test marks, which are themselves geared to such training.

This parental unhappiness, however, makes life difficult for private school administrators. The board members of schools started in outrage at the actions of courts or public schools or society in general, tend to distrust professional school administration credentials. So they hire headmasters without much background and then are dismayed when problems develop. When that dismay overflows the headmaster is the first to go, which makes, Bills suggests, a certain tension running right down the hierarchy.

---

*The Bills' report, which makes up Part II of this book is quoted purposely from time to time when its points seem particularly to refresh Part I.

THE SCHOOLS THAT FEAR BUILT.

46

7

The Physical Qualities

Most of the new schools are small and rather dismaying in appearance. They are in irregular buildings that often are ill-kept if not dirty and inside and outside they lack most of the equipment that has come to be considered standard in modern American schools.

There are exceptions, of course. The most outstanding building among the new schools seen by the Society's investigators certainly was that of Briarcrest High School in Memphis. As might be expected from its $6 million cost, its size, quality and equipment are consistent with a first quality school anywhere. The Hammond Academy in Columbia, South Carolina, named for a prominent South Carolina family, has excellent facilities, as does Northside Baptist Church Christian School in Charlotte. But the fact that such examples are exceptions indicates the quality to be found in most new schools.

More often, the exceptions are in the opposite direction. One small Christian school in Memphis once housed a failing Bible college; one in Atlanta still is cramped into a small Bible college. In at least one case in the "massive resistance" period a private school opened in a public school building that had hurriedly been declared surplus and sold. Schools have started in old stores and abandoned manufacturing plants. Many have begun life in private homes. The Council schools of Mississippi opened first in a private home before moving to a newly erected building. Growth into a full-fledged system is unusual in private schools, but most of those started in homes expand or fail. If a school is not strong enough to get its own building, it probably is too weak to survive.

The new schools generally appear in two types of buildings. Many are in churches or church auxillary buildings intended primarily for Sunday School classes. Others are in all-purpose buildings, often modular and often of metal, which have been adjusted to classroom needs. The two forms often are combined, since this is the kind of building a church is most likely to choose when it expands its school, which typically comes in the second year if it comes at all. It is a further measure of building standards that these essentially temporary buildings appear as a great improvement—fresh, clean, new, with rooms of adequate size—beside the church building already in use.

Such buildings are quick to go up and can be torn down readily if necessary. They are designed for multiple uses and it is simple to equip them with partitions generally the size of standard classrooms. They also lend themselves to the kind of free labor available to so many schools from the pool of parents. Such buildings are cheaper to buy, cheaper to erect and easier to finance because of their potential conversion to other uses.

Even the well-financed Council school system followed this general concept. Its school buildings are of good if modest quality which have been placed geographically and designed internally so as to be converted readily to general business use should the school venture fail. This was reported to have been a condition imposed by financing banks. The actual form is a series of small buildings each holding two classrooms and linked by covered walkways. In the event of failure, these schools won't stand empty, as closed public schools so often do. Of course, it follows that a building readily convertible to various business uses is not likely to be as effective for school use.

Most southern churches are solid structures, usually made of brick and frequently rather dour in architectural concept. The idea that the classrooms included in these buildings for Sunday School purposes convert readily into regular classrooms is deceptive.

Sunday School classes are traditionally small. They are taught by lay people who are in good supply and who function best with a small class. Many Sunday School rooms are built in units of one small room with three closet-sized rooms attached, so the class may divide still further. Often these rooms have no windows or only one small window, indifferent lighting and poor ventilation. Many are furnished only with a little ring of chairs and lack blackboards or other equipment. But they are only to be used for an hour a week.

It usually is expensive to convert these areas into regular classrooms, and most churches make the move under economic pressure. Walls are knocked out to expand rooms, lighting is installed, new ductwork for heating and cooling appears. Frequently there is an untidy and unfinished look, ductwork not closed off, wires dangling from conduits, testament to volunteer labor. When rooms are painted, which often they aren't, they tend to be in unusual colors, the result of using donated paint. Even after renovation, the rooms usually are small and often oddly shaped, some with no windows and many with small windows that seem to block contact with the outside.

The schools often look dirty. Few have full time janitors. Floors usually are swept, but cleaning woodwork seem beyond the resources of most schools visited. Sumter Academy in Sumter County, Alabama, has a small building on the outskirts of York, Alabama. On the day the project visited it, the halls were dirty and in one place dirt had been swept into a pile in a corner and a broom left standing against the wall. The furniture was battered, the walls inside and out were in need of paint and scattered around outside were dilapidated house trailers that may once have been used for instructional programs.

Supplies and equipment seem always short and of poor quality in the new schools. Most use furniture cast off by public schools, graven with generations of initials. Rooms often have a barren look, with a single blackboard and a small bookcase holding a few readers. Walls are decorated according to the teacher's energy and ingenuity and often the rooms have a dowdy, uncomfortable feeling with old, odd-sized furniture and bare walls.

Slide and film projectors and tape players are rare. So are map cases and globes. Art supplies are scarce. Few rooms have a dictionary larger than a paperback on the teacher's desk. Laboratories for chemistry and physics in high schools seem particularly bare. Often there is a single experiment table with sink and Bunsen burner around which students cluster. Better schools have a small table for each student and a shelf full of cheap microscopes, but the resources of the laboratory remain limited.

Most limited of all and traditionally the most difficult to build is the library. Most schools have set aside a small room for books and the better ones have a book buying budget ($2,000 a year at one of the better new schools in Charlotte). Most schools start with a tiny donated nucleus of books that often are quite irrelevant. A Christian school in Atlanta, for example, has fewer than 500 books that include bound volumes of *Popular Mechanics* and a handbook for tearing down a 1952 Ford. Sumter Academy's library was in a converted classroom and included devotional books that were common in theological schools three and four decades ago. Most of these donated libraries are weighted with pious books that offer more exhortation than information. Most have picked up an old encyclopedia somewhere. But even the biggest and best schools, some with professional looking libraries full of empty shelves awaiting books, concede that starting a library all at once is painfully expensive and difficult.

Parents come in and cook a hot lunch daily at a few schools. Briarcrest High, always the anomaly, has a milk shake machine and a grill for charbroiling hamburgers. But the common facility is a collection of machines that dispense soft drinks, milk, cookies and candy to supplement the lunch the child is expected to bring to school. There are all kinds of machines, too. At one school, the headmaster said proudly, "You see, there's never an excuse for a child to be without a pencil. He just puts a quarter in the machine . . . " Among other things, the remark was indicative of the general affluence of new school patrons.

New schools are likely to move toward a gymnasium as their first big building project and many churches already have gyms (for their youth activities program) when they start a school. Gyms are popular with students, but they are even more popular with supporting parents who seem to revel in old fashioned school spirit around basketball teams even more than the students. Most communities boast athletic conferences for Christian schools. Academies in Jackson, Charlotte, Atlanta, Memphis and many other places play in these special leagues; Briarcrest has become so strong it dropped out of the Christian league for lack of competition and now plays public secondary schools. Most gyms seen by Society investigators were standard and adequate, though their very presence often was disproportionate given the overall scale of the school.

Outdoor facilities seem sparse. Most church schools have little more than a basketball hoop suspended over the parking lot (which usually is big enough for the whole congregation but is only used on Sundays). Occasionally one sees playground equipment, but it is rare to see a track, hurdles, a baseball diamond or a football field, even at schools with adequate land.

The thing which one does see outside the new schools are rows of yellow school buses waiting to return the students to homes all over the city.

Southern states make few demands on private schools beyond fire safety and adequate sanitary facilities. States publish the standards they set for public schools, but even the best of the private schools rarely bother to try to meet them. Briarcrest's elementary system, for example, is all in suburban churches. "We don't try to meet state construction standards," an official said, "We use what the host church has."

The better of those new schools which include high schools are interested in accreditation, though there is an increasing feeling that this has become less significant for college admission. This seems especially true for students who make high SAT scores, and the new schools tend to focus on training that can be measured readily. There also is an increasing feeling among new schoolmen that they are becoming sufficiently powerful in a political sense that institutions of higher learning would prefer to avoid any inference of discrimination against them and thus are more than ever willing to rely on the anonymous score.

For most new schools seeking accreditation, the biggest barrier is library shortcomings (most have adequate teachers and the nature of the curriculum is not an issue in the accrediting process). A number of the bigger and better of the new schools are in the self-examination process and by the time of this book's publication a few may have achieved accreditation. Some new schools vehemently reject the whole idea of accreditation as another interference with their concept of freedom. The issue thus takes on political overtones, though casual observation suggests that the schools most likely to reject the accreditation concept are those least likely to achieve it.

In summary, the new schools range from structurally adequate at the top of the line down to places that don't deserve the name school. Most of the new schools are dilapidated, worn, a little dirty, short on supplies and materials, cramped, offering few opportunities for enrichment. They are, in short, the very sort of places that would enrage taxpayers if offered to children by the public schools.

8

The Teachers

The new schools have no trouble attracting qualified teachers and holding them despite pay scales markedly below those of public schools. The new school movement has coincided with the national oversupply of teachers, and applications roll in when word of a new school appears. Many come from afar. Most administrators enjoy showing a sheaf of applications awaiting an opening. "I was amazed at the response from teachers," one pastor said. Sometimes there is an element of fervor. When Citizens Against Busing opened 26 schools in Memphis, it reported some 15 to 20 teachers working without pay. It is evident that whatever the National Education Association thinks about the new schools, many public school teachers in the South see them as entirely reasonable alternatives to public schools. As a result, most teachers in the new schools hold degrees and are reasonably well qualified.

An Atlanta headmaster, noting the teacher oversupply, said he gets calls of inquiry constantly and that about a third of them are from teachers already employed in public schools. Many of the teachers in the better new schools have come directly from public schools, where among the rank-and-file there seems to be powerful support for the new school concept. Public school teachers are much more likely to reflect the attitudes of their clientele than of higher level administrators. A recent survey, for example, showed that half the teachers in integrated situations don't agree with national integration goals. They often see themselves in the front lines of enforcing social change that they don't like and there is considerable resentment in their ranks. Many are frightened of new and different kinds of students, especially black youngsters from ghettos who arrive at formerly all-white suburban schools. Considering the more diverse student bodies in today's schools, the emphasis on student rights and reduction of autocratic discipline and the requirement for imagination on the part of teachers imposed by modern curriculums, teaching in public schools is more challenging than ever and a good many teachers don't find that challenge pleasant.

Joe Clayton, Briarcrest High's principal, an old public school man himself, thinks that teachers are relieved to come to his school from city schools. They find it less taxing, more traditional, calmer. "It is a much better atmosphere here," he said. They are back among their own; there is less fear, less culture shock, more comfortable homogenity. Many public school teachers in Bible Belt communities are themselves members of fundamentalist churches and are likely to be in full sympathy with the philosophic thrust of the new schools. Principals of new schools often describe with satisfaction the fact that they have students whose parents still are teaching in public schools. Many echoed the sentiment of one who said, "Most teachers still in public schools would like to get out, but they can't afford the salary cut or to lose the retirement rights they've built up. But their decision not to put their own children in public schools pretty well tells the story."

Thus most of the new schools have an adequate supply of qualified teachers. They are likely to be fairly young, either new graduates or people with so little time in public schools they have no stake in staying. Many new schools expect to get their new teachers from the next graduating class of the nearest state college. Some make it a point to seek graduates of small Bible colleges as likely to be more philosophically in tune with the school. Teachers are likely to be certificated in at least one state, though often they are not certificated in the field in which they actually teach nor are their degrees in that field. At one elementary school, for example, all 24 teachers were certificated, four had master's degrees, one had 18 years experience and there were 50 strong appllctions for the 10 positions that would be open the following year. Quite possibly these figures are deceptively high, however, for Professor Bills found an overall lower level in his more systematic analysis of 11 specific schools. The following comments are from his report:

"Four per cent of the teachers do not hold degrees and about 80 per cent hold only a bachelors degree and are frequently teaching in fields in which they have less than minimal preparation. About 17 per cent of the school personnel hold masters degrees and less than one percent hold a sixth year degree or have completed two years of graduate study. These findings can be interpreted to mean that the teachers are poorly qualified when compared with teachers in the public schools.

"Headmasters are also poorly qualified. The highest degree for one headmaster was the bachelor of divinity, another held only a bachelor of science degree. The remainder of the headmasters and principals held masters degrees, often in fields other than educational administration. One headmaster held the doctor of business administration. Only one school had both elementary and secondary principals; the remainder had only the headmaster, administrator or principal.

"Twenty-one per cent of the teachers were in their first year of teaching and another 21 per cent had only one or two years of previous teaching experience. Twenty-two per cent had three to five years of experience. Thus, about two-thirds of the teachers had five years or less experience. These statistics are based on the report of the headmaster.

"Twenty-one per cent of the teachers were less than 25 years of age, 26 per cent were between 25 and 30 years of age, 23 per cent between 31 and 35, 23 per cent between 36 and 50, and 7 per cent were above 59. Thus, in comparison with the public schools, the teaching faculty is young.

"Only about 85 per cent of the teachers are certified or qualified to be certified as teachers in some state at the minimum level. The remainder are not qualified. Of the qualified teachers, many are teaching out of field." (see pp. 110-111)

Pay scales are definitely lower than in public schools, but most new school people feel that the lowered pressure of teaching in their homogenous environment makes up for the pay shortage. One principal, whose pay scales ranged from $5,900 to $7,500, said bluntly: "They don't care about money—their husbands are working." Most new school teachers, it seems, are married women whose salaries do represent additional income. The lowest pay scale the Society encountered was a flat $5,000 for 10 months. The most common figure was a little above $6,000 for starting teachers. The Briarcrest elementary teacher starts at only $5,800, though high school teachers draw considerably more. The highest starting salary the study encountered was $7,500, which approached public school scale in that city and may have accounted for the headmaster's claim that he had about 10 applications for every position. Many schools are willing to reward experience; one that begins at $6,800 runs up to $9,980 for 14 years experience and a master's degree. Almost invariably, salary is calculated on and paid over a 10-month period. The school with the lowest pay scale also was the most fervently religious of all the project encountered. "Money isn't the issue," the headmaster said. "I look on teaching as another ministry. I don't suppose I've ever hired a teacher who asked about salary."

Christian schools expect teachers to be "born again" Christians, which means that they have gone through a personal, specific individual-to-God experience in which they have accepted Jesus Christ as their savior. This, in fundamentalist doctrine, is the mark that separates those who are saved from those who are not, and it has nothing to do with mere church attendance or membership. "If they've had this experience, they know it," one principal said succinctly.

This is made a flat condition of employment. "We tie it right down in our application," a principal in Atlanta said. "We get it in writing." But the query doesn't stop with the application. At Briarcrest, Principal Clayton said he regularly interviews prospective teachers and draws out their conversion experience. "They have to convince me that it's genuine, that's all there is to it," he said.

The idea behind this requirement is practical enough. These are Christian schools and they handle all subjects in a manner that is consistent with fundamentalist doctrine. Teachers are expected to witness to their faith in the classroom and to draw on faith as a basic perspective for viewing most knowledge. "We are a Christian school," one principal said, "and if you have no faith to share, well! When a child asks, we want the answer to come right out from a basis of knowing the teacher is sincere."

Some of the schools go a good deal further in testing the qualities of potential teachers. Their elaborate application forms take on political as well as theological aspects, and the nature of the questions and the statement of faith give an interesting view of the school's outlook. For that matter, the willingness to interrogate prospective teachers on deeply personal beliefs and to require them to sign doctrinal statements says a good deal about the school's view on matters of individuality and personal rights. Thrifthaven Baptist School in Memphis is especially severe. Are you now, its application blank asks, or have you ever been a Communist or Socialist? A homosexual or pervert of any kind? What is your attitude toward the American Free Enterprise System? Can you explain the difference between a republic and a democracy? Between "progressive" and "traditional" education? How do you feel about the "Jesus Movement?" About the cooperative evangelism of Billy Graham? Do you believe the Genesis account of creation (creation in seven twenty-four hour days) as opposed to evolutionary theories? Then it set out the following doctrinal statement. Could you sign it, the application queries. "If so, sign it; if not, state what part you cannot adhere to and why." It continues:

The Bible. Verbally inspired (that is, EVERY WORD was given by God). Literally true and infallible, including the statements concerning biology, history, creation, the future, etc.

Jesus Christ. The Son of God, born of a virgin, died for the sins of men, rose bodily from the dead, and ascended into Heaven.

Man. Every man is naturally depraved, devoid of any spark of divinity, and totally incapable of any good through his own efforts or desires.

Atonement. By the shed blood of Jesus alone. The law of God imposes a sentence of punishment upon a sinner. This sentence was executed upon Christ when he died. He substituted for us.

Salvation. By Grace through Faith in Jesus. An instantaneous, supernatural rebirth of the soul. There is no other way for man to escape damnation for his sins.

Security. Once saved, a person can never be lost again. The believer is eternally kept by the power of God Himself.

Baptism. By immersion only, following salvation. Baptism has nothing to do with salvation, but is the first step of obedience in a new Christian's life.

The Future. The imminent and premillennial return of Jesus Christ. Eternal joy in a literal Heaven for all who have trusted Christ, and eternal, conscious torment in a literal, burning hell for all who have not trusted Christ.

Secular schools put less emphasis on the specifics of faith, but otherwise their outlook and requirements of teachers seem strikingly like the Christian schools. The secular school is less likely to hire only "born again" Christians; but neither is it likely to hire anyone who would be uncomfortable in a Christian school.

The emphasis of this discussion has been on teachers, but principals are cast generally in the same mold, share the same beliefs and enforce the same standards. Many principals in better schools have had public school experience, often as a teacher rather than an administrator. They often are older people, sometimes coming out of retirement to get a school started, and they tend to have fond recollections of what public schools once were, before, as one put it, "they started going to the dogs." It is an unusual school that can afford to hire a full time principal. Most teach as well, many looking forward to the day when they can take a half-day for administration.

9

Bible-based Schools

The new Christian schools are Bible-based. The secular schools are less focused specifically on the Bible and religion. They are likely to have chapel once a week and to have daily prayer with the pledge of allegiance, but not to have Bible training. Yet as we have seen, the outlook of the secular school, its approach to society, its attitude toward education, its political views and the nature of the education it offers is so like that of its sister Christian schools as to make them indistinguishable except for the latter's overt religious bent. In this chapter, therefore, we will treat them as one, with the proviso that religious questions apply more clearly to—but are not limited to—the Christian schools.

Bible-based means that the school turns in every particular around Bible teaching and interpretations. "We simply take the Bible as the basic rule of authority," an Atlanta principal said. "Faith in the Lord is the beginning of wisdom."

"If the Bible and a textbook differ," said the principal of one of the more extreme schools, "we know the textbook is wrong, and we teach children that. For example, we show what's wrong with the evolution idea. We teach the theory of evolution as a system of error. God's word won't allow more than 10,000 years, and probably it's more like six to eight thousand. We expect the teacher to explain the bias of the writer, which is important because, of course, we must use some humanistic texts. There just aren't that many really Bible-based texts."

As we have seen, regular Bible study, usually of "the Bible as literature," is required in the Christian schools, as is regular prayer, devotionals and chapel. At the latter children often are invited to throw down their depravity and be saved. No students are excused from Bible study and chapel, which indeed go to the basic concept of the school, if not its primary purpose.

Often parents are asked to sign a statement accepting religious training (as opposed, however, to proselytizing for the particular division of faith sponsoring that school). The school that demands that at least one of a child's parents sign a statement of belief, uses the same statement it requires of teachers. There is little room for dissent in such a school. One pastor noted an interesting side effect to the training. "I'll tell you," he said, "some of our Sunday School teachers are finding themselves tested by the new knowledge of the Bible that the kids are bringing from the school."

The same attitudes permeate the approach to subjects. "The whole trouble with public schools today," said one pastor, "is that you can't bring affirmative testimony about God sending His son to save men. They don't know anything if they don't know that, you see."

As the teacher is expected to be willing and able to witness to the faith in the classroom, so the teacher is expected to keep a weather eye cocked toward the Bible itself. Mathematics regularly is taught as key to the structure of order in God's universe. "Science from a Biblical viewpoint is exciting," one headmaster said. At one school the study of spelling and grammar begin with the idea that God invented language in order to be able to converse with Adam in the garden, that He then gave it to men so they could talk to each other and that it therefore behooves the student to use correctly this tool of God.

Rosemary Hatcher, principal of Shively Christian School in Louisville, described it this way: "Everything begins with the presence of God. God is the creator of us and hence of knowledge and truth and this is what we teach. In math—it's not just numbers, it's the orderliness of God's handiwork. It's not just happenstance that numbers fit together as they do. And when you get to light years and the nature of the universe, why it is all God's work. And history—history is not unrelated things that happened to happen. We see it as the unfolding of God's dealing with man. God is in control. He allowed some to rise and caused others to fall. God has told us what to do with our lives and here in history we can see what happens when we fail to live up to his word. God warns that when people hit a low moral point, destruction follows. Look at the Babylonians, the Romans . . .

"Well, the Civil War is a little harder to teach in Biblical terms. But we would teach the facts. Of course, many people do believe a curse was put on Noah's son, Ham, and he was told he would find himself subservient to his brothers. And slavery was an issue in the Civil War. And you can see the Bible was right. Black people have been held down. But God is a respecter of persons—He never wanted people to own others. So there were good reasons for the war. The point is that God is in control—what happens in the world is not just happenstance. . . "

The teaching of the theory of evolution is, of course, the great sticking place for Christian schools. "Science and social science are so permeated with evolution and humanism that we must be sensitive to the dangers on a day-to-day basis," said one principal, who described his school as "dedicated to helping Christian parents save their kids." Even at Briarcrest, a model of moderation among the new schools, the elementary principal notes that "we depend on teachers to put the Christian factor in place," and the high school principal says that on the evolution question, he checks out the science teachers in advance. "We believe and we teach that man was created by God, and not derived from a monkey or any other source. We don't mind discussing theories, but I say to my teachers, 'Don't you let those kids get away without knowing what we believe.' "

Mrs. Rosalyn Rose teaches biology at Briarcrest. She is a gracious woman with a master's degree who spent fifteen years in public schools. She was a little wary and said immediately that the evolution issue really didn't arise—the kids just weren't interested. She explained it all from a Christian viewpoint and that was that. But what would she say if a student stood right up in class and pointed out that most scientists accept Darwin's theory? At that Mrs. Rose bristled and snapped: "I'd tell them that most scientists have an atheistic view."

At Elliston Baptist Academy, Oscar Ammer said, "At first the preacher didn't want it taught even as a theory. Then the science teacher talked to him and they worked something out." Rather stiffly, Pastor Simmons said, "I would have no objection to kids knowing the evolution theory. It is a farce."

"Students should be aware of the theory," another headmaster said, "but we would take a strong pro-creationist stance." At Northside in Charlotte, a teacher observed that evolution simply is taught as a "false doctrine." And the headmaster in Atlanta summed up his feelings this way: "We teach evolution, put it in perspective. Science is theory, you see. The Bible is fact. When God says He made things a certain way, that is a fact. When a scientist says you come from an ape, he is crossing man and beast, which the Bible says does not happen. We feel the facts are there to be seen. The world is as the Bible describes it. And we bring in outside resources, people with a scientific and an evangelical background, and they put it all in perspective for the kids."

Beyond religious questions lies political conservatism, which often clashes with modern textbooks, and which marks the new schools indelibly. The great cleavage between fundamentalism and the modern liberal view turns on the question of man's responsibility for and to his fellow man. Since the fundamentalist view is that man's salvation depends entirely on faith, it resists books that equate goodness with social responsibility. The theme common in many books on social studies that society has a duty to provide for its unfortunate members and that the provision is a right for them to enjoy is rejected. At the same time the mood of questioning of old values and of celebrating change that has come upon America strikes no resonance in these schools. Books that deal directly with racism that is a canker on American life or that recognize the fallibility of American foreign policy or that look tolerantly on internationalism find no favor.

"We have a history that praises the United Nations," Mrs. Hatcher said, "but our board here feels that the U.N. is not at all good. There is a book praising Martin Luther King. We find books knocking the forefathers. They weren't perfect, they were human—but why tell third graders that? People need heroes."

In her doctoral thesis on the subject of private schools, Margaret Rose Gladney quotes a southern independent school leader's view on the problem with modern texts:

> Current textbooks project an unrealist image. These books depict a homogenized, egalitarian society not consistent with the background of our students. Our pupils come from homes where individualism and fixed moral values are stressed. We need to devise textbooks projecting an image consistent with our national and southern interests.

This reaction to modern textbooks is not limited to the new private schools, of course, but its strength there helps identify the outlook.

Once past these ideological flashpoints, however, the curriculum in the new schools seems predictably dull and limited. Most schools use books from the state-approved list of texts. Some use castoff books from public schools. Some states require the use of at least some books from the central list. In any event, it is an unusual school in which books from standard publishers make no appearance. Most of the new schools do supplement their textbooks with those from the line published by Pensacola Christian School and others in the burgeoning Christian School supply business which is discussed later. Often used in the schools for supplemental reading, these books usually recast familiar material from an evangelical viewpoint. As the number of new schools makes publishing for them profitable and more publishers enter the field, many headmasters say they look forward to the time when the new schools can rely entirely on Christian publishers.

Whatever books they use, their approach is spare if not bare. Elementary schools teach reading, writing, arithmetic, a little social science and a little physical science. They put great emphasis on reading and use old-fashioned rote techniques. They follow a phonics method and some have reintroduced the McGuffey Reader complete with its archaic illustrations.

In spelling, arithmetic and reading they put much emphasis on drill which produces high test scores, and it is on this basis that they claim their superiority to public schools. Given the approach, they are almost certain to improve a child's score and thus to satisfy his parents. All the teachers and headmasters the project interviewed felt without qualification that this was the key to good education and that the lower scoring they said they encountered among children coming from public schools was the mark of bad education. At a small school which by most modern standards would have to seem hopelessly inadequate, the headmaster said proudly, "Our kids are getting six years of learning in three years. It's easy. You don't have to have miracle teachers or superkids—but there's no fooling around. 'Old Hickory' sees to that." He uses phonetic reading with a great deal of drill, and puts most of his emphasis on reading. "By the time they're out of kindergarten, they're reading—some at the fifth grade level." His subjects are Bible, English, social studies, math and some science when they reach the junior high school level.

"I call it no frills education," said Mrs. Archie Van Buskirk, principal of the Frayser system in Memphis. "What do I mean by frills? Lots of extra things you think it takes to make kids happy. Extra art work and so on. When I say basic, it's not just the 3 R's, but the focus is on the academic. I'm a language arts person and I believe if a child can read in the first three grades, the rest of the skills come along." She then went on to cite a respectable list of standard text-books of the sort that are regularly used in public schools.

The Frayser system is a distinct cut above most schools encountered in the study, but it is a fact that the new schools generally turn the "no frills" argument to their advantage. They insist that public schools have become so immersed in frills, incidentals and ir-relevancies that they have lost touch with plain old fashioned education. Lowering test scores in public schools are seen as proof of this argument. The new schools' attention to basics, to reading and figuring, with time devoted to drill instead of to broadening the student, thus is turned into a virtue that is reflected by increased test scores. Smugly, some new school people like to assert that for half the cost they can deliver twice the education by their attention to basics. The broadening or enriching qualities which one might feel a modern world demands of a modern curriculum are dismissed as time wasters that implant "wrong" ideas in student's minds anyway and are contributing to a decline in the quality of American life.

The no frills approach becomes a cover excuse for the absence even of "old fashioned" enrichment—music, art, varied athletics, shop, business skills, drama, speech, debate, etc. Except in the biggest schools, foreign language courses are rare. Schools with some musical facilities orient to church music and focus on instruments like the guitar or whatever a teacher of some other subject happens to be proficient in. The result of all this is that the child with special talents or interests which might be awakened or developed is left unattended. Skills that a more sophisticated school system might find and expand as a matter of course remain dormant unless the child has the strength and interest to acquire them on his own.

In high schools, the problems are compounded. Elementary school, after all, is much less demanding in personnel and range of subject, and among the new schools, elementaries far outshine high schools except for the few exceptions like Briarcrest. Most new schools add high school only under the pressure of students who want to attend and often add only those grades for which students apply. One school, which opened with 198 students had 65 in high school, of whom one was in the 11th grade and two were in the 12th. All three left after the first semester and the school then was much more comfortable with only two years of high school. It planned a third the following year to accommodate students it hoped to retain.

Under such circumstances the range of curriculum the school can offer is painfully limited and usually consists of English, math, science and social studies which include history and Bible. If a teacher happens to be available and equipment can be found and there is room in the school, they may occasionally offer courses in typing or home economics, though the teacher is likely to have those duties added to courses already being taught. High school teachers often are expected to handle more than one subject area and often there is more than one level in a class. If one teacher, as is quite common, is handling all science and math classes, obviously there must be doubling up.

The economic pressures on the new schools fall most severely on high schools, which are considerably more expensive in any education system. That probably is why the quality of teachers is most likely to fall off in the high school level of the new schools. In the upper classes of one newly opened school, for example, English is taught by a retired minister and science and math by a man trained as an engineer.

In his report on the 11 schools he analyzed, Professor Bills took a sharp view of the curriculum examples he encountered. The comment is drawn from his report:

A principal inadequacy is the curriculum of the schools. None of these schools have enough teachers to provide real choices in a comprehensive curriculum. Even in the large school described above the teacher/pupil ratio was 34:1 indicating a restricted choice. That school did offer music and art which is absent in many of the schools but required courses in religion of all children, thereby further restricting choice. Although many of the schools claim general education as one of their goals, the only choices available to students are in driver education, typing, and type of mathematics. Most students take English, mathematics, history, and science plus one additional course. The full range of mathematics is offered in only a few schools and in others even the restricted range is made possible by alternating algebra I and plane geometry in successive years. Physics and chemistry are likewise alternated. Several schools further reduce choice through required religion courses and time available for scheduling courses is reduced by compulsory chapel exercises each morning. In several instances it was noted that to give children a choice of classes, a class might contain students from grades 7 through 12. In most schools the range was somewhat less but it is not uncommon to find at least three grades represented in one class. One direct result of the restricted curricula is the claimed concentration on college preparation. Presumably such a choice reduces the necessity for a varied curriculum. (see pp. 109-110)

10

The Financial Side

Rather than there being more than meets the eye in the finances of the new school, there turns out to be less. There is nothing mysterious about the capacity of the new schools to start, survive and even flourish at the very time when private education was in trouble and considered by many to be doomed by economic realities. The study began, of course, with that question: how is it possible and does it imply some unusual funding source?

The answer turns out to be quite simple and straightforward, and the Society's investigators are confident that it is correct. It comes in two parts: first, the schools live successfully on their tuition; second, they can do so because they keep costs low in a variety of ways.

Every school works out its own tuition charges and each is different, but most come out in about the same place. Most offer a reduction for additional children from the same family and some have a top figure beyond which no single family need pay regardless of the number of children. Some church schools will accept tithing (before taxes) to the parent church as a substitute for tuition payments. Most schools require annual payments; some accept payment by semester.

Occasionally one finds a school charging as little as $400 a year for elementary tuititon, but most charge at least $500. The most common figure one encounters in looking at many schools is $600 a year for the first student in the family. Briarcrest, for example, charges $650 a year for elementary schools, $550 for each additional student from a family. High school charges usually are higher: Briarcrest High charges $875. In the eleven schools Professor Bills studied, tuition ranged from $450 to $900.

Speaking generally, then, a tuition range of $550 to $800 would cover almost all of the new private schools. When Citizens Against Busing began its rash of schools in the post-busing hysteria of Memphis, it charged $350 for the first child from a family and $150 for each additional child from a family. CAB's proprietors feel today that the charge was too low and was one cause of their speedy collapse. Tuition charges at most of the new schools have risen in the last two years and some public school experts feel that this limits their attractiveness and growth potential. If costs continue to rise, some new schools may price themselves out of their market.

Five hundred dollars a year would appear to be the lower limit on which a school can survive and most schools that last take a firm, business-like view of the matter. "You have to have money to run a school," one principal said, "and if you're lax you're probably going to close."

"We demand tuition in advance, when they register," one pastor said. "Some people ask if they can pay half and half, and we usually allow that. We give families from our sponsoring churches the first right to enroll, at which time they must pay, and after July 1 we open enrollment to the public. We'll help a family arrange a bank loan, but we won't reduce our fees. Lots around a church gets done on sentimentality, you know, but in the school business that just won't work."

The parents, as it turns out, can afford these figures, or at least, enough parents to keep the schools alive and running. Obviously, as in the case of the Bartons mentioned earlier, it works hardships on a family with more than one child. But while not many of these parents are actually wealthy, it appears that most of them are comfortable. They are in business or are employed in white collar or skilled blue collar jobs. Professor Bills found that about half of the families supporting the eleven schools he studied made more than $15,000 a year, and it is the casual impression of the Society's other investigators that the income picture for most parents supporting the new schools is somewhat higher than that. So while the payment of these tuition figures implies sacrifice, it tends to be sacrifice of luxuries the family might otherwise have, a newer car, a boat, a vacation. Frequently the wife in the family will get a job or a part-time job to pay for the tuition. One parent observed, "Why I couldn't pay that tuition in a lump sum—I don't have that kind of money. I take a note at the bank every year and pay it out." But the real point in his observation is that he has a steady income and has no trouble meeting the note payments.

School proprietors tend to be slightly contemptuous of the idea that their parents suffer. "It doesn't strain people," one pastor said. "They're pretty affluent around here. They cut out the extra car, that's all." Another said bluntly that the school makes no provision for helping parents, nor does it think in terms of scholarships. The Council schools in Mississippi insist that their tuition ($700 a year for elementary and $850 a year for high school at last report) "are within the means of 98 per cent of the prospective clientele."

Schools that see themselves as a public service are more inclined to be lenient. Rural secular academies that see themselves still as *the* school for whites in a county usually will not turn a student away, though they are likely to set up scholarships which wealthy people in the community quietly fund. This is the practice in the academies in both Sumter and Greene Counties, Alabama. At Elliston Baptist Academy, Pastor Simmons says that he isn't in the collection business and that he expects to lose some $14,000 a year in tuition that isn't paid. Since he accepts tithing as an alternative to tuition, genuinely poor people can send their children to the school at less than the usual tuition rates. The defunct CAB schools also accepted "hardship cases."

So, generally, parents can afford a tuition figure that rarely is more than half the per-pupil cost in public schools—and the new schools can survive on that figure. The nature of the Society's project did not lead to inspecting a school's account books, but so many cited the same general figures in discussion as to preclude much possibility of error or hidden factors.

The schools survive because they keep their expenses low. They consistently pay teachers well below scale and profit from an over-supply of teachers. At the same time they accept less than fully qualified teachers and even more important, they use amateurs, volunteers, part-time people or retired people to round out the bits and pieces of their curriculum. They have fewer services in general. On only one occasion did a project member encounter a school nurse. Few have full-time librarians. Coaches teach courses and principals usually teach and administer. Janitors are usually part-time. The fact is that the schools offer bare bones education at a bare bones price.

Most schools also have low capital investment costs because so many are in existing church buildings. Even those that must expand are able to do so on church property and often the church will pay for the new building from its own resources. Few churches charge rent for their buildings. In the Briarcrest system, for example, there are 13 elementary schools in various neighborhood churches. The system pays utilities and custodial care but no rent.

Secular schools lack the advantages of a supporting church, but the buildings they raise are consistently inexpensive. Often they take advantage of an existing building which can be bought or rented at a minimum figure. This is the point, incidentally, when gifts do come into play. Many schools conceived in religious or political fervor find that land is available at unusually low prices or that the owner of a building will give or rent it for a minimum price. At the Frayser system in Memphis, for example, a pastor observed that when they decided to buy land on which to build a high school, "we were able to buy it at $6,000 an acre—until then it had been offered at $12,000." He went on to suggest that this was God's way of helping the school and assuring its operators that they are on the right course, but it is possible to see it in more temporal terms. A secular school started in Charlotte in the wake of *Swann* began looking for land on which to build and was given 9.53 suburban acres by a member of its board. "He said he had inherited the land," the director of the school said, "and he knew this use would have pleased his daddy."

The Council schools were given 17 acres on the city's outskirts in the early period and a wealthy family in Charlotte gave a whole building to one of the better schools there.

The other great reducer of capital costs is the supply of free labor among parents on which new schools draw. Working bees turn out at nights and on weekends. Many members are skilled laborers. Plumbers, electricians, building trades workers, air conditioning and furnace men ply their skills. Some can call in friends to assist who are not otherwise connected to the school. These people usually can get supplies and equipment for a new building at or below cost, using a combination of their business connections and the same fervor that leads to land offered at less than market levels.

And, of course, there are gifts from within the church and the community that make up deficits. Pathway Christian School in Atlanta, for example, ran into problems when it made some administrative mistakes, and had a budget of $99,920 against tuition income of $61,200. Gifts made up the difference. The school has about a hundred students.

Even with plenty of volunteer labor, it still is necessary to raise a good deal of money to get started even in a small way. Shively Christian School in Louisville, which is anything but overendowed, got up to $50,000 in a few weeks to pay for remodeling the church building and other costs in converting to a school. The Frayser system's new high school in Memphis will cost $500,000 without the gym, which is to go up later. It is assembling a plant for 1,800 students at surprisingly low cost, but still will have an investment approaching $1,000,000.

Some of these schools become big business. Briarcrest expects income of more than $3,000,000 from its near 4,000 students which explains the confidence of the bankers on its board that it can retire handily the more than $4,000,000 it owes on its big new combination high school and church building.

When a school plans construction that runs into the hundreds of thousands of dollars, there has to be a funding source. Briarcrest used banks, as do most church operations. Middle class churches of any size have tremendous fund raising capacities within their own membership. East Park Baptist Church is not unusually rich but neither is the $1,000,000 it raised at its "faith pledge picnic" unusual. From time to time churches do go broke, but the more common event is that a church outgrows its building and floats a million-dollar loan to build a new one. Banks have been supporting such construction for years and extending their confidence to the church's desire to build a school is just a small additional step.

Secular schools lack the organizational structure of a church, of course, but a few strong figures in a community can supply all the confidence a bank needs to make a construction loan.

Large operations sometimes turn to bonds. The Frayser system, for example, issued $700,000 in 9 and 9½ per cent bonds maturing in up to 15 years. It published an 18-page prospectus and recently had sold all but $200,000 worth. Southern Baptist Education Center, also in Memphis, which is owned by a consortium of ten Baptist churches and has 1,270 students in a handsome new $2,000,000 building on a 36-acre campus, floated two bond issues. The first was for $900,000 and the second for $1,200,000. Parents of students, naturally, are the obvious purchasers of these bonds. There was a bit of a flap in the summer of 1975 when the school told parents it might not open if they didn't buy more bonds. In the next ten days $230,000 came in. The bond, of course, has an additional effect: once a parent has invested in a bond, he has a financial interest in seeing that the school succeeds. SBEC has designed a further income source: when a child is enrolled his family must put $1,000 in escrow where it will remain with the school using the interest until the last child in that family graduates from high school even if they leave the school (the money is refunded if the family leaves the Memphis area). This gives the school interest income in the neighborhood of $1,000,000 a year.

As the new school movement has grown, supplying it has become big business. There are brokers and financial advisors, for example, ready to help a new school issue bonds or stage fund raising rallies. Many successful new school operators offer assistance and advice in starting schools. Some regard it as an extension of their ministry—secular or Christian—and some combine it with business. The Council schools boast of the number of schools they have helped start, and the headmaster of a big system in Memphis makes it a regular practice to travel around the country offering advice and instruction. Shively Christian School at Louisville began with the assistance—financial and advisory—of Robert Thoburn, proprietor of the successful Fairfax Christian School of Fairfax, Virginia, which began in 1961 and now has nearly 600 students. Thoburn came to Louisville with a manual, "How to Establish and Operate a Successful Christian School," which Don Grice relied on in opening his school just two weeks after making the decision to start it. Thoburn also has a publishing arm which produces textbooks consistent with the views of the Christian schools.

Probably the leader in the Christian school curriculum business is Pensacola Christian School which was founded in 1954 and now has more than 2,800 students. It recently opened Pensacola Christian College as an extension of its school and has an elaborate publishing arm called A Beka Book. Perhaps the most important part of the Pensacola package is a curriculum which instructs the teacher what to do and how to do it on a day-by-day basis for the whole year. A competent teacher might find this constricting but it comforts a neophyte or untrained teacher. More important, it allows a pastor who knows nothing about a school to start one and have some sense of what he should be doing, what his teachers should be doing and what he should hope to accomplish. These curriculum plans sell for $100 per grade and can be used again each year.

The popularity of curriculum plans that eliminate the need for pedagogical knowledge on the part of those who start the new schools indicates the quality of many of the schools. Pensacola probably is the older of those developing such plans, but it has competitors. The men from Dade Christian School and Gold Coast Christian School in Florida have combined to offer a program they call CS-80 (for Christian Schools 1980) which is beginning to offer a range of textual material and a daily curriculum. Schools using the materials also engage the consultative help of the CS-80 staff. It is somewhat more expensive than Pensacola's materials.

A Texas firm, Accelerated Christian Education, offers a total package in a non-graded, non-formal classroom approach. Each child works at an independent carrel and proceeds at his own pace with occasional direct instruction from a teacher. The child studies books and workbooks provided by ACE and at least one school using the system manages to hold twelve grades in only two classrooms with teachers handling students at various levels according to need. In a copyrighted statement, ACE describes its approach:

Teacher lectures, textbooks, and work assignments are replaced by "Action Curriculum Educators:" a combination package of recorded cassette lecture, text and workbook . . . each packet consists of approximately one month of sequential programmed work in Language Arts, Mathematics, Science and Social Studies . . . the student listens on a cassette while he reads along in the information section . . . The key to achievement is *controlled progress learning* with built-in incentive and adequate motivation.

On actual examination, the material seemed sketchy and carried a distinct conservative political bias.

All of the systems depend on fundamentalist Christian ideas and all insist that in addition to sound education, they operate from a Bible-based, Christ-centered viewpoint. Within the evangelical faiths, however, there are radical differences of opinion on education forms. Dayton Hobbs, who runs a Christian school at Milton, Florida, attacked ACE recently in his newspaper, *The Projector*, observing, "'Individualized instruction' is one of the latest humanist methods whereby the student teaches himself without the assistance or with very little assistance from a teacher . . . the philosophy is that the 'child is basically good' and is able to instruct himself . . . (as opposed) to the truth that the child is a depraved sinner, unable to know what is best for himself and must be inspired and motivated by the teacher . . ."

Pensacola Christian has systematized its approach to starting new schools and offers seminars on the subject. Its vice president is A.A. "Buzz" Baker, a bright fundamentalist who once was a professor at Bob Jones University in Greenville, South Carolina. Bob Jones incidentally, also is a mainstay to the new school movement. Its graduates are scattered throughout the schools and the 1,000 students in its School of Education (total enrollment in the university is 5,300) provide a constant source of new teachers. Bob Jones was started half a century ago by a famous evangelist of that name and it stands largely alone, unaffiliated, a thriving institution at the zenith of conservative fundamentalism.

Buzz Baker travels constantly around the country, carrying the word of the possibilities Pensacola Christian offers. He regards his work as a form of ministry. "If we can help you," he tells people interested in starting Christian schools, "we feel we have a share in your ministry forever, and that's what we care about." Then he tracks them through the basics of opening a school in their church. He assumes they have the building, tells them where to find furniture cheaply, how much to charge for tuition, how to set up bookkeeping, where to find textbooks and what they should seek. Academics is the key, he says, that's what parents seek, so get a good academic program. Pensacola holds a three-day clinic for principals every year; at the eighth clinic, in 1975, there were 314 attending. The school also holds an annual clinic for teachers.

Public school, Baker thinks, is awful, dedicated to humanist principles, not godly at all. "Some of these kids we get for just one year," he warns, "so we had better do a job on them—training them for the Lord." He describes Pensacola system starting with kindergarten with complete teacher schedules and lessons the teacher follows all day. "You can do the same—you have everything we have learned after 23 years." Reading starts in kindergarten, heavy on phonics, and continues right through the grades. "The greatest ad you have is satisfied parents. Kids go home reading, and believe me, parents are excited. You have these little phonic cards. When the child learns to read the little card you give it to him to take home. And what does the card say? 'See the sun? God made the sun.' If you're going to teach them something, let's teach them something that counts for eternity. And they read it to the parents and of course the parents are excited.

"Kindergarten is the key. It gets them started right. And have a kindergarten graduation. They love it. A guy in Indiana told me he had twelve graduates and he raised a crowd of 290 people. It's a great interest raiser. Have a kindergarten diploma—it's terrific promotion, and people wonder what this could do for their fifth grader."

Baker urges them to build a base. Open with K, one and two, he says. Next year, have two K classes, one, two and three. Third year have three K classes, two one's, two two's, a three and a four. And so the school builds, growing from the bottom, generating its own clientele for the upper grades. People will want a high school immediately; fight them off if possible. Have full classes. Look at the economics of teachers. It costs the same to have a teacher teaching ten or thirty kids—thirty is the class size to aim for. What do you look for in teachers? Teachers with a bent for the ministry. That is what we offer, a ministry; we don't pay much but we offer a ministry. And don't pay them much; keep the tuition low and then more students can afford to come.

You too, in other words, can start a school if you like. Pensacola's curriculum, which the school's catalog now claims is in use in more than 1,000 Christian schools, takes "the guesswork out of teaching," in Baker's phrase. It also explains the capacity of little churches that have given no prior thought to education to spring to life schools that at least have the appearance of legitimacy. And, with Pensacola Christian School's extensive publishing interests, it also becomes a sizeable business.

11

The Clientele

The youngsters who go to the new schools and the parents who support the schools seem to love them. "Lots of our kids have talked their way in," one headmaster said. "I mean, they hear about it from their friends and they visit and then they go home and persuade their parents. I had a boy in here today. He wants to drop out of public school, though he's a star football player and by coming here—conference rules—he'll lose a year's playing. He talked to me a long time and then he said, 'well, I'm going to go home and try to talk my dad into it.'" Such youngsters, of course, have real reason to try to excell when they enter the new school.

Professor Bills' study of eleven schools puts its emphasis on how students perceived the schools and felt about them and how parents reacted to them. It offers systematic analysis of the results. What follows in this chapter is casual observation made on a non-systematic basis in a large number of schools all over the South. It happened to match quite closely Professor Bills' findings.

For the youngsters, the schools seem to represent homogeneity, solidity, comfort, reinforcement of ego, a sense of being part of an elite. Almost invariably kids in the new schools have come from public schools, and the Society's investigators found none who did not think that what they had left behind was vastly inferior. They talked of the tranquil study atmosphere in which it was easier to learn, and gave the impression that there was much less anxiety here than in public school. They described fewer fights and less reason to fight.

The students insist that they learn more, must study more and feel demands on them are greater. This may be, though most of their learning turns around drill, which seems harder at the time but makes less intellectual demand. The work results in measurably higher scores which then reinforces their feeling of achievement.

The homogenous quality obviously plays a big part in their approval of the school. Everyone here is as they are, from similar background, operating from similar assumptions, competing in the same framework. There is considerable comfort if not much challenge, in such a situation.

The fact that their parents support the school and warmly approve of it seems to have a reinforcing effect with the students. Popular myth may overemphasize the rebellion of youth; as one moves through the various new schools, one is struck again and again by the pleasure and comfort the students there find in their parents' approval. If they do well in this school they stand higher and more securely in their parents' eyes.

Perhaps the other side of this coin is that these are coercive schools which act as extensions of parental value and influence. A youngster who was in real rebellion against his parents might find the atmosphere in a new school too stifling to stand; there may be a natural factor that selects out those who would be uncomfortable and leaves ever higher mixture of those who reflect and can be expected to perpetuate their parents' views.

The parental approval and the willingness of people to make real if not cataclysmic financial sacrifice probably grows from essentially the same points. The schools reinforce and even certify their outlook and their social view. The schools stress discipline, order, old fashioned learning and religious values at a time when people of this outlook see change as a dangerous tide threatening to overwhelm them. Again and again, both parents and the operators of the new schools talk in terms of these *real* schools, the kind they remember from the past, the way public schools used to be.

And there is another point, more subtle and rarely addressed directly, but certainly part of the equation. The schools stress the idea that obedience is a Biblical injunction. They stress a line of obedience, from government to the people, from school administrators to students, from parents to children.

They teach obedience to parents as a primary commandment. They teach respect, parents often say, but rarely add for what; in fact, the respect the schools teach youngsters is *respect for parents*. In an age when parents often seem to have trouble commanding their children's respect on their own, that is a comforting coercion from the school.

The new schools draw their clientele largely from people who share their basic premises. Parents and students seem fully comfortable with the religious focus of the Christian schools. But religion does not seem to be the motivating factor in patronizing the schools. Professor Bills reported that about two-thirds of the parents queried in his study said they patronized the schools because they believe their children learn more than in the public schools. As one principal put it, many parents who "fled busing hadn't realized what a Christian education could do for their child." George Barton, describing his considerable sacrifice with warm approval, put the whole weight of his pleasure in having three youngsters in Briarcrest not on Christianity or on what they were learning or on the school's philosophy, but on his own peace of mind. "It's worth it," he said, "it's worth every penny, knowing they're there, knowing they're all right."

12

How Good Are
the Schools?

This report has tried to let the realities of the new schools speak for themselves, and the attitudes of their proprietors emerge in their own words. The judgment of the academies properly is the reader's, but it also seems appropriate for the researchers to offer an assessment.

First, how good are the schools? The answer appears to be that despite the claims of their proprietors and the satisfaction of their patrons, by modern standards they are not very good. Now that modern public school buildings have become consistently excellent, it has become fashionable to sneer a little at the attention the law pays to the child's physical environment—how many toilets per hundred children, how much light, how much noise? But all these points were written into standards for public schools in many states because they are important. And across the board, from too few toilets to small windows and poor lighting to inadequate playgrounds to cramped rooms to collapsing, mis-sized furniture, the new schools generally are uncomfortable and depressing places, considering that a child spends a major part of the year in school.

Though the new schools try to make a virtue of their limited curriculum, in fact it is limited. The new schools can manage almost no enrichment and even standard courses often are offered in alternate years, with several grade levels squeezed into a single class. Many of the new school teachers are trained well enough, though they tend to be young and inexperienced, but there are enough former ministers and other non-professional teachers in some academies, particularly the smaller and newer ones, to pull down the average.

New school people boast uniformly that their schools are better than public schools, but that certainly seems a dubious assertion. They are much more homogenous than public schools and undoubtedly more tranquil, but they find it difficult to show that their instruction is superior. Most base their assertion on the high scores in reading and other subjects which their students achieve. Obviously these are a measure, but they don't appear to be the only measure and there are several factors to be considered.

First, the new schools tend to draw from public schools only youngsters from a socio-economic class that implies, on the average, a better home atmosphere, a higher ratio of families with mothers and fathers living together and other indices that are associated with achievement in school. Second, since the schools are generally new, the youngster now making the high SAT score in which the headmaster takes such satisfaction actually was trained in public school for years before coming to the new private school. It is all very well to talk of merit scholars, but those in the new schools who win the scholarships give the impression that they would have done so in any school they attended. Third, the focus on phonics and other drill procedures mean that the new schools stress a relatively narrow area of learning which happens to test well. The schools test reading ability, but the don't test philosophical outlook or the capacity to interact with society or grasp of the individual's place in the world. Even the argument for the importance of basics doesn't hold that only basics are important. Furthermore, it isn't entirely clear that test scores in the new schools are so different even on basics. A researcher in Memphis tested the first hundred students alphabetically in a private school and a comparable public school and found that although the highs and lows of the reading scores in the public school were more volatile, the two schools averaged within a point of each other. The private school refused to allow the researcher to publish its name. Professor Bills found that the students in the eleven schools he examined were not much different than those in public systems in the South that he had tested previously.

The new schools damage public schools, though how much is not clear. The new schools are much smaller in percentage than the public schools—"Does the mosquito destroy the elephant?" asked one new schoolman. And probably the success of the new schools is more clearly a symptom of the damage in public schools than a cause. But the haven they offer fleeing middle-class families certainly exacerbates the problems in public school. As the more stable element departs, the proportion remaining becomes more and more volatile, which provokes further flight. In time the public schools could become essentially pauper systems educating only the disadvantaged. Considering the nature of American society, the disadvantaged are likely to be disproportionately black. In Atlanta, with the black middle class fleeing right along with the white class, educators in the 87 per cent black system now say openly that they are serving a new clientele which has different needs and requires different approaches.

Meanwhile public support for public schools is fading. The perception that leads some people to private academies is shared to at least some extent by their neighbors. The more that public schools are seen as black enclaves, the more white voter support falls. Voters are increasingly snappish about taxes and they have been turning down bond issues relentlessly over the last decade, particularly in the South. Memphis' school budget was slashed recently and it is not alone. Most state aid to schools is on a *per capita* basis and shrinks as enrollment shrinks. But in an equation that unfortunately is much less evident, falling enrollment doesn't mean falling costs. This is especially true when the students left in the system have a disproportionate need for special programs.

Surely whatever erodes support for public schools is dangerous. In an ever faster, more complicated, more technological society, representative democracy relates directly to education. If people are to make wise public decisions—and for that matter, if they are to survive at all in such a society—they must be educated. And for the mass of the people, that means public education.

But society's needs aside, the new schools also seem to be unfortunate places for their patrons, so little do they offer students living in a modern world. They seem narrow and insular at a time when human perceptions are widening. They are homogeneous when the pluralism of the American society is newly apparent, and they are separatist when we already are polarized politically, racially and even rgionally. Their self-satisfaction is monumental when the rest of society is questioning itself and seeking new directions. They mistake old attitudes for old virtues, looking backwards as we hurdle forward. Indeed, they seem withdrawn, as if by recreating in their tight little enclaves a society in which an earlier generation felt comfortable, they can make today's world go away. But really, that is nicer for parents than for their children.

For it is in the real and changing world that their children will live. The effect of the tranquil and somewhat sterile island of the schools is to sever its clientele from the pluralistic society around them. College may re-insert some of the new school students into the ongoing society, but the high school student moving from graduation directly into the workplace seems likely to arrive with skewed notions of the nature of the world.

As they attempt to perpetuate the past, so the new schools perpetuate old attitudes, old fears and old hatreds. The story of the South for the last three decades had been one of awakening, expansion of ideas, amelioration of old hatreds. In any people, this process moves best from generation to generation; children do, in this sense, instruct their parents. But the new schools enshrine parental attitudes and may well have the effect for their students of severing this generational expansion and maintaining attitudes and outlooks that the rest of the society is setting aside.

Finally, the segregationist academies are destructive to what is a central question before the American people today—whether we are to remain two societies or become one. The academies were founded to perpetuate separatism. They stand as havens from integration and association with other cultures and colors. It is on this point that the schools are most of all antithetical to the course upon which the American society has set itself.

Part Two

The Analysis

By Robert E. Bills

This section is a specifics-oriented analysis of eleven particular segregationist academies in several southern states and the attitudes of their students.

1

Focusing on the Schools

During 1974-75 eleven "newly developed" private schools were studied to provide information on their characteristics, their problems, and their effects on children enrolled in them. Two of the 11 schools were located in South Carolina, four in Georgia, three in Alabama, and two in Tennessee.

Selection of the Schools. The schools in the study do not represent all of private education; not even the full range of private education which has developed in recent years. To begin with, an attempt was made to include only those schools with grades 1 through 12 or kindergarten through 12 (although one school inadvertently was included which had only grades 8 through 12) and only those schools which had come into existence within the past ten years. Furthermore, no recently established school was selected from religious groups which have a long history in parochial education such as the Roman Catholic and Episcopal churches. If anything, the schools may be somewhat above the average for the group they represent; however, the range of the 11 schools is such that they give an excellent idea of the variability of such schools.

In the initial phase of the selection process use was made of a list of the 100 largest school systems in the United States whose school population is 30 per cent or more black. Of these 100 school systems,

16 are located in the south and seven in the seven-state area covered by this research project (South Carolina, Florida, Georgia, Alabama, Tennessee, Mississippi, and Louisiana). These systems were Memphis, Atlanta, Mobile, Birmingham, Caddo Parrish (Shreveport), Muscogee County (Columbus(Georgia, and Charleston County, South Carolina. An effort was made to obtain one or more schools from each of these seven cities. This attempt was generally unsuccessful. The final list of schools includes two from Memphis and one from Birmingham.

tacts. Three of the 11 schools in the project entered the project on the basis of personal contacts. The first two of these three schools were tested, reports were made to the schools, and permission was secured from the headmasters to use their names as references in seeking other schools.

At this point a letter writing campaign was initiated and 204 personal letters were written to schools in the seven state area and an additional school was sought through personal contact. As a result of the personal contact, the project director was invited to visit the school and to explain the project to the faculty which reacted enthusiastically. However, the faculty decision to participate was overruled by the headmaster with whom the original contact had been made. It appeared that he had hoped the faculty would veto the idea.

The letter writing campaign resulted in requests from 25 schools (about 12 per cent) for further information. Of these 25 schools, eight decided to participate, one agreed to participate but withdrew on resignation of the headmaster (not related to participation in the project), two agreed to participate but at too late a date for inclusion, and 14 made no further contact. All of the eight schools which agreed to participate as a result of the letter writing campaign made such decisions following telephone contacts with the first two schools which were tested.

Method of the Study. When a school agreed to participate, three things were mailed to the headmaster: 1. a copy of an information schedule which he was asked to complete, 2. a rating sheet for each teacher, and 3. copies of the Teacher Problems Q-Sort which he was asked to administer to the faculty. The rating sheet for each teacher asked the headmaster to rate the effectiveness of the teacher, the teacher's area of greatest strength, and the teacher's area of greatest weakness. The Teacher Problems Q-Sort is an instrument which is completed by the teacher, either in a group session or at the teacher's leisure, and which describes the most pressing problems of the teacher. The instrument gives a measure of the teacher's openness to experience.

A mutually convenient time was arranged for a visit to the school. Such visits extended over a three-day period. On the afternoon of the first day, the project director or Dr. Lewis Blackwell visited with the headmaster and then met with the faculty members to enlist their cooperation in the testing and to give instructions about how the tests were to be administered to the students.

Students were tested on each of the following two mornings. The schedule of tests were: First day, Feelings About School and the Relationship Inventory; Second day, Locus of Responsibility Scale and Index of Adjustment and Values. On the first day of the testing students were given a copy of the Parent Inventory to take home and to return the following day. Parent Inventories which were returned late were mailed to the project director by the school. Descriptions of each of the instruments are given in later sections of this report.

Other data consisted of the observations of the project director of Dr. Lewis Blackwell and graduate assistants (if any) who helped conduct the testing.

Data for each school were analyzed and a comprehensive report was given to each of the schools. In two schools these reports were given to the faculty by the project director. Reports were mailed to the other nine schools.

In testing students, teachers, and parents, all members of each group were included. The original intention was to sample each of the groups and to take a pre-determined minimum from each group. However, to give greater reliability to the data, to assure cooperation of the schools, and to be of as much help as possible to the schools, complete groups were tested.

It is not possible to determine the extent to which the reports will be used to improve the schools. Feedback from the headmasters has been excellent and it appears that as a group they are as interested in using the data as other groups which have been tested in a similar manner. The greatest interest of the headmasters appears to be in the Parent Inventory. These schools are most responsive to their parents.

Reasons for Participating. Reasons for participating in the study varied from school to school. In the three schools which participated following personal contact, an important reason for participation was to help the project director; however, at least two of these three schools desired the data and appear to be using it to good advantage.

Most of the schools desired to participate to prove to some group how good they were. Usually this group was the board and the most useful instrument for this purpose was the Parent Inventory. One headmaster participated to gain information with which to fight his board. It was his intention to show the board that his methods had produced significant results. Unfortunately, his data were of little value for this purpose.

One reason stated by several schools was that they desired that their students participate in standardized testing whenever possible because of the practice effects. It is known that the more opportunity students have to take standardized tests, the better they score, other things being equal.

At least four of the schools, including the two mentioned above, participated in an effort to help their schools improve themselves and with the belief that the data would prove helpful for this purpose. All schools were permitted to examine all test material prior to making a decision to participate—had they not had such an opportunity it is doubtful that any of them would have participated.

In one of the above four schools, the headmaster stated that he was glad that some group was finally interested in aiding the private schools by making available such a testing resource.

It is not known why one of the schools participated. This head-master said in advance that is was doubtful that the instruments would be of much help to his school since they seemed to be based on a philosophy of government education and his school had a philoso-phy of Christian education. He wrote the project director following receipt of the report and restated the same position but added that the Parent Inventory seemed to be the most helpful instrument—he would reinterpret the findings on all other instruments in light of his philosophy of Christian education.

Interest in taking the tests and in faculty participation varied from school to school but appeared to be about the same as in most schools with which the project director is familiar. One school is worthy of special note. More copies of one instrument were discarded due to obvious lack of interest on the part of the students than has occurred previously in any school. In this same school the Parent Inventories were returned in the poorest condition of any school to date.

Reasons for Not Participating. In general, the schools which did not participate gave few reasons for their action. Some of these schools did give reasons and some who participated expressed their anxieties in a variety of ways, giving clues to factors which entered into their decisions.

The headmasters of most of these schools appear uncertain of themselves and highly insecure, although exceptions exist. Those who are most secure are well-prepared, experienced public school personnel whose first concerns are for the quality of the educational experience provided the students.

In many ways the question was raised, "Are any government (federal) funds involved in the project?" Had such funds been involved it is doubtful that 10 of the 11 schools would have participated. When it was explained that the funds originated from a foundation it was asked, "What are the purposes of the foundation," and "What are the sources of its funds?"

Although the headmasters in most instances have the option of including testing programs in their work and are charged with responsibility for efforts to continue to improve the schools, in almost every instance the headmaster sought the approval of the board before proceeding. This appeared to be occasioned by the presence of the Parent Inventory in the battery. In several instances the board withheld permission. There appeared to be a fear of what the results of the testing would show and of the uses of the results.

Many of the headmasters appeared to feel that participation in the project might "rock the boat" and that all things considered it might be best not to participate. The short tenure of the headmasters in these schools indicates they may have reason to be fearful. Those who did participate seemed to be of two types: those who consider themselves to be good public relations people who could use the results to their own advantage and those who were sincerely interested in improving the schools. Unfortunately, only three or four of the 11 headmasters appear to fit into the latter category.

The Headmaster's Insecurity. Insecurity on the part of the headmasters in these schools appears for a variety of reasons. As will be seen later in this report, these schools are highly responsive to their patrons and these patrons do not agree any more with each other about what a school should attempt to achieve than patrons in most other types of schools. As a consequence, the headmaster is caught in the middle of a number of opposing forces, all of which have a direct and important voice in the conduct of the school.

Partially as a consequence of the above, the tenure of the average headmaster is short. But the short tenure results from other factors. In the initial phases of developing a school, there are many financial problems and many of the headmasters are poor business people. Many of these schools have no plans for long-range debt retirement and in others the plans are vague. In at least one instance, a system of these schools was established as a "holding action" until the people could have time to amend the Constitution to erase the problem which was the cause for forming the school. Since such action was not forthcoming the system folded.

In other instances, the cost of the schools is considerable in relation to the income of the parents. As a consequence, parents are unhappy and believe they are subjected to double taxation—they support public schools, but they must pay additional for their "own" school. The headmaster may feel the brunt of this unhappiness if any budget increases are sought.

A more important reason for the headmaster's short tenure lies in the unrealistic ideals the founders of these schools have for the schools. They often start with assumptions such as: the public schools are inadequate because of the quality of the students who attend them, the public schools have poorly prepared teachers who do not concentrate on correct teaching procedures and who are poorly prepared, almost any good business man could do a better job of managing the schools than a school administrator, and almost anyone can do a better job teaching and administering a school than teachers prepared in schools and colleges of education.

Such test data as are available in the schools indicate that the children are markedly like those found in most public schools (with the exception that no black children are included). IQ's appear to range from about 85 to about 125 and are not those of the exclusive preparatory schools parents frequently desire. Many of the parents have assumed that their children are not achieving in a superior manner because of the inadequacies of the public schools. When their children fail to achieve better in these even more inadequate, developing schools they begin, again, to blame it on the school personnel and the headmaster.

Another factor which accounts for the short tenure and the insecurities of the headmaster is the changing role concepts of those who are responsible for these schools. In most instances these schools have been formed to avoid something—usually integration (although most are reluctant to admit this). Since the original problem supposedly was solved by the formation of the school, the parents now become more concerned about what is happening to their children. They begin to aspire to higher achievement for their children, to higher "Christian" values, to higher education at an exclusive and prestigious institution, and to other new goals. As a consequence they desire the school to change. But change is difficult. The school has developed a debt problem and has problems meeting its payroll. To achieve what the parents desire would require a considerably expanded faculty and a faculty of higher quality than that available. Plant and equipment improvement would be imperative. For these and other reasons the school cannot satisfy the demand and the headmaster is fired.

Furthermore, the headmaster may not have been prepared for his job. Some headmasters are ministers, others are businessmen, and some, although educators, have had no training or experience as school administrators. In fact, in only three of the schools the administrator had college preparation for the job prior to accepting it. The headmaster is forced, because of the shortage of money available for teachers' salaries, to employ teachers with little experience and sometimes with inadequate preparation. As will be seen, the teachers in these schools are young and have minimal preparation. The most effective administrators are those who have had special preparation for the position and who are experienced in the job.

Not infrequently the headmaster is presented with a divided board—some members believe the school should develop in one direction, others in different directions, and some have no idea of the direction. The boards have poorly defined role concepts and frequently formulate policy *and* administer the schools.

Although what has been said to this point might lead to a conclusion that parents do not like these schools, such is not the case as will be seen from data presented later in this report. The parents like the schools—they own them, the schools are responsive to them, and the schools present "solutions" to what the parents perceive as catastrophic problems for their children. The picture, though, is often far from a pretty one. As do most parents, the parents of the children in these schools have, on the average, high ideals for their children. These are usually "Christian" ideals or ideals of academic excellence which are exaggerated to the point that it is obvious that parents, and sometimes school people, see the children as a means by which they can re-live their lives in the lives of the children. Naturally, there is no questioning of the goals or of the ability of the children to achieve these goals, thus, the fault must be in the school.

The public schools have obvious inadequacies. One of these is their lack of responsiveness to parents. But the heterogeneity of the students, their parents, and the school personnel prevent using (exploiting) children to the degree it occurs in some of these private schools. In this sense, the lack of agreement among parents of public school children is an asset to their children.

Like all schools, these exist to mold children. The difference is in the direction of the mold, which in the new academies is in the direction of an ideal sought by the parents and frequently by school personnel. At the same time these same people have accused the courts of using children to solve social and other problems through "rewriting" the laws. If this is true, is it not also true that parents are doing the same thing to their children in these schools?

Quality of the Schools. The quality of these schools seem to vary directly with the number of children who qualify for admission and whether or not a school has the backing of influential members of the community. If there are enough children to support a school (which must be at least multiple sections of the same grade), a more varied program can be offered and some standards of achievement and discipline can be maintained. A small number of students means that even if one child drops from the school the budget may be out of balance. If a school cannot be selective, it has low standards, poor parent support, and high tuition. Only one of the schools had a selection program for students and this school rejected only the lower seven per cent of applicants and this was done on the basis of the Otis-Lennon test (a paper and pencil test) of intelligence.

Many of these schools do not have a large pool of children from which to draw and so their quality is poor. As an illustration, one of the 11 schools enrolls more than 90 per cent of the "eligible" children and has only 240 children in grades 1-12. Furthermore, the school is in a rural area and the parents are unable to pay the higher tuition rates necessary for a quality program. Another school is located in an isolated area of a large city. Residents of the area are lower middle class and upper lower class whites, and it is surrounded by residential areas with high percentages of black people. The limited enrollment of the school permits only one teacher per grade, including the high school grades. It is doubtful that this school can ever achieve quality.

The problem of securing sufficient children for a balanced curriculum leads many of the schools to concentrate exclusively on college preparation even though there is evidence that only a small percentage of the children will seek to attend college. In one school which concentrates on college preparation, the headmaster sold one set of parents on sending their mentally retarded child to his school because he would "be made fun of" in the public schools. This school was not prepared to deal with the problem and it failed to help the parents understand that the public school their child would attend had special facilities for working with the child. This same school prides itself on the nature of its "Christian" philosophy.

If a school survives its initial period of formation and increases in size, it can employ better qualified personnel, purchase better equipment, become more selective, have a more varied program and thus improve its quality. *Other things being equal*, the longer a school has been in existence the better quality it may have. However, enrollment trends show that some schools decrease in size as they age and that the average school rapidly reaches its maximum size and does not increase thereafter.

There are many factors which contribute to the quality of a school such as the school plant, the curriculum, qualifications of teachers, equipment, and others which will be discussed in later sections.

One problem is related to the inadequate pool of prospective students and consequent poor financing of the schools. This is the problem of discipline. In some schools the discipline is excellent; in most it is poor (discipline is used here in the sense of order, not in terms of the aggressive, hostile, and other negative behavior which exists in some public schools today). In some of the private schools there is a fear of reprimanding children because of parents' reactions and possible loss of tuition. Children often are present in the halls of some of the schools and it is difficult to determine in some schools when the day begins and ends. In one school it took 20 minutes to settle down to the task of taking the tests, in another the time was 45 minutes, and in some, children were in the corridors throughout the testing periods. One school resorts to "in-school" suspension of students meaning that the student who is reprimanded must attend classes and finish all assignments for a predetermined period of time but he receives "zeros" in all classes for that period of time.

2

Characteristics

Although generalizations can be made about the schools, it must be recognized that each school differs dramatically from all of the others. This uniqueness is the result of adapting what is present in the community to the financial resources of the schools.

For example, one school occupies a 300-acre campus that is beautiful and well-kept. Its five buildings have a feeling of permanency and the new ones are well-planned. The school dates back a number of years but was a small boarding school until 1969-70 when it began to grow at a rapid rate because of integration of the local schools. At the same time the school signed the compliance provisions of the Civil Rights Act and became eligible for Title I and II support including support of its lunch program. Its president is a minister who also is the administrator of the school, but the school is under the direct control of a well-qualified principal who is young, energetic, prepared as an educational administrator, and an experienced public school teacher and administrator.

The principal, in turn, is assisted by two experienced professionals who had graduate training in educational administration. One of these people serves as principal of the high school and the other as principal of the elementary school and as the guidance person. Teachers in the school are better prepared than the average and have more experience. They are well above the average age for teachers in these schools.

The school is located on the outskirts of a large city and has an ample pool of students from which to draw. There are relatively few financial problems and the school is able to maintain high standards of discipline and dress.

Even this school is not free from problems. In particular it has inadequate science laboratories and its library lacks basic reference materials. A school uniform is required of the students which consists of plaid, pleated skirts for the girls, worn with a white blouse and red sweater or blazer with the school emblem. The girls wear red socks with two tone saddle oxfords. The length of skirt is a continuous problem although little is said about it; it is finger-tip length but the girls raise their shoulders when being measured. The boys dress in gray flannel trousers with white shirts and red blazers or sweaters. The trousers suffer during recess periods. The school has an especially strong art and music program.

The above school is highly atypical for the group although another of the schools has moved into the campus of a defunct girls college and occupies the administration building which has been converted into classrooms and office space. The original library and laboratories of the college are available to the school. The plant is valued at $2,500,000 and the school has spent $45,000 in renovations. It currently rents the building and has an option to purchase the campus with rent applying to the purchase price. Unfortunately, the information sheet was not returned by this school and the cost of tuition and other fees is not known but must be considerable.

At the other end of the spectrum is a school which began in a residence and then moved to an abandoned public school building (rent free) before it discontinued operations when forced to leave the building. It reorganized itself when a building which had formerly housed a garment factory was donated to the board. This building is a one-story, corrugated steel building in the shape of a "U." It has double-loaded corridors with a low level of illumination. The building is poorly ventilated because of its small, swing-out type windows, and because of inadequate window space its classrooms are poorly lighted. Each classroom is equipped with a window air conditioning unit which is too small for the load. Classrooms are heated by gas heating units suspended from the ceilings.

The floors of the buildings are brown, asphalt tile squares on concrete. These tiles give the appearance of never having been scrubbed or waxed. Since there is no janitorial service, the floors are dirty and dust is abundant. There is a "clean-up" period of 10 minutes at the end of each day when the children pick up paper and sweep with brooms. Play space consists of one-half of one acre although there is an adequate athletic field one block away and there is an attractive gymnasium.

The boys's rest room on the high school side of the building has two commodes and four urinals. One commode was stopped up by the roll of toilet paper which had been dropped into it. Neither commode had a hanger for the toilet paper.

The drab, depressing atmosphere presented by this building which resembles a dark, temporary, World War II building is not enhanced by the used furniture brought to the school from its previous place in the public school and augmented by poorly made tables and chairs. The lunchroom furniture resembles homemade picnic tables.

The headmaster holds a bachelors degree and the faculty is equally poor in its qualifications. Two of the high school teachers do not hold a bachelors degree. All teachers, with one exception, are female.

School starts gradually. The headmaster was to arrive at 7:30 to open the building to the examiners. He appeared at 7:50—school supposedly began at 8:00. Teachers continued to arrive and two of them appeared at 8:10. Children dragged in until 8:30.

At 8:45 grade 8 sent for six pencils. They had not started testing at that time. The reason was discovered later. The children were selling magazine subscriptions for the parent-teacher organization to help finance the school. The quota for each grade was $300. Grade three had raised $52 and was in difficulty. The parents say that they bought the magazines last year and do not want them now. There were definite signs of pressure. The specific purpose of this project was to purchase lockers—there are none in the school.

It was learned that at 8:30 the headmaster had made an announcement on the inter-com (the library speaker was shut off) asking the salesmen to return to their rooms so that the testing could begin.

The gymnasium is a separate building which the school constructed. It is a pre-fabricated, steel building of modular construction. The shell for such a structure can be erected in about 10 days.

About one-half of the children bring their own lunches. The remainder eat in the cafeteria which serves hot dogs, hamburgers, french fried potatoes, potato chips, etc. The cafeteria is "manned" by a parent taking a weekly turn.One parent each week takes responsibility for purchasing and preparing the hot dogs, hamburgers, and french fried potatoes. Elementary children may purchase milk although "coke" machines are available.

There is no art or music in the curriculum. One room apparently was once used for art. There is a large, practically unfurnished teachers lounge and work-room. At one time it was probably a classroom. There are no tables in the elementary wing—the furniture is used, one-arm, moveable chairs which are arranged in straight rows. The library has home-made tables and wooden, folding chairs which were probably donated by some church after it no longer had a use for them. Library desk tops are unfinished, hollow-core doors.

The children were frequently left unattended in their classrooms after the testing. They were amazingly quiet, in fact they appeared apathetic. The headmaster reported seeing children in town at midnight and later on school nights. One examiner asked a bright eyed fifth grade girl what time she had gone to bed the previous night. She informed him that it was around 9:00 and when he asked what time the other children in her grade went to bed the answer, "Usually around 11:00."

Attendance was poor on both days of the testing. Several of the students were absent attending the Master's golf tournament. A local two year college was having its annual feast day which consisted of drinking beer, eating, and dancing until late at night.

The school draws about 90 per cent of the "eligible" children in its geographical area and has only 240 children in grades 1-12; thus, it does not have a bright future. Parents send their children to the school because there is no other private school, and they can not or will not send their children to the public schools which are integrated. There are four such private schools within a 40 mile radius.

Several parents did not complete the Parent Inventory and said they would not do so. According to the teachers this was because the parents were suspicious and thought individual returns would be checked. The headmaster was observed "auditing" classes over the inter-com.

This was the only school in which the information schedule, teacher ratings, and Teacher Problems Q-Sort were not ready on the arrival of the examiners and they left without the information schedule and rating blanks but with a promise that these would be mailed. The examiners made it clear that processing of the data could not proceed without all of the data on hand. Two follow-up telephone calls were necessary to receive the information.

Uniqueness and Opportunities. The schools have a freedom which is absent in the public schools, but they fail to capitalize on it. A primary role for these schools could be in experimenting with new methods of educating boys and girls. Instead they are inferior copies of traditional practices.

Part of the opportunity of these schools is in their informal atmosphere. In most the faculty members smoke as they desire. The male librarian in one of the schools smokes while he takes care of the library. He also smokes in class when he teaches. Yet smoking on the part of the students is not a problem. Furthermore, the schools are not restricted by law and can permit smoking. In most, students smoke in rest rooms and outside the building if they have permission from home. In some schools (the "Christian" ones, in particular), smoking is prohibited.

The informal atmosphere results, in part, from the size of the schools; the smaller the school the less formal it is. In many there are no inter-com systems and the teachers and headmasters are pleased with the arrangement. Because of the absence of such a system, there are supposedly fewer interruptions of the classes.

The beginning of the day in most of the schools is casual—the schools do not start on time. Likewise, the schools take breaks during the work-day to suit their own convenience.

The informality of the schools is illustrated by the manner in which a student request for access to the faculty coffee urn was handled in one of them. Such a request was made and the coffee was made available. Only five or six students bought coffee at the 10:00 a.m. break. Gradually the number decreased and there were no purchases. The urn, which had been placed in the lunchroom when the request was made, was removed and returned to the faculty lounge without resistance. There were no such requests the following year.

In one school, with parental persmission, students did not have to attend study halls. It is believed that classes are so small that if students are not prepared, the faculty will know and will take measures. In another school, study halls have been dispensed with and children may leave campus with parental permission. Such freedom should be an introduction to the greater freedom of college and acceptance of responsibility.

In most schools excuses to pass from one place to another are not necessary and the teachers are not forced into a role of policeman.

Buildings. As already indicated, generalizations about buildings are difficult to make. The most frequently appearing structure is the prefabricated, modular, steel building which can be erected on a concrete slab and which takes only a short time for completion of the shell. In erecting such structures, the slab is poured and then the assembly crew arrives with the building on several flatbed trucks and with a moveable crane. A large structure can be completed within nine to ten days. Completion of the inside structure varies with the funds available and in some instances can be comfortable and attractive. Such buildings usually have no windows so that all lighting is artificial and it is necessary to provide air conditioning. Such schools are finding the increasing utilities rates to be burdensome.

Another popular structure is the concrete block building with a poured slab floor. In general these buildings are less substantial than the modular, steel structures and one such building is experiencing many large cracks and leaks. These buildings frequently have modular, steel structures built as an addition to house the gymnasium. All of the schools, except one, have large gymnasia as central aspects of the buildings.

Many schools have not had the funds available to build elaborate structures during their first years. One school has already been mentioned which was housed in a residence, moved to a public school building, disbanded, and reorganized in its present, permanent, garment factory building. Another school existed four years in a residence before moving into its concrete block building. Another school was started in the education wing of a church and has since expanded into two residences and has recently built a modular, steel main building and a separate symnasium of similar construction. Another school, which has recently built a cinder block building, started in a motel. The second year it moved to a building which had formerly housed an automobile agency. It has now expanded into its new building but kindergarten through grade 6 are still housed in the former automobile agency.

Building sites vary considerably in adequacy. The large campus already described for one school is more than adequate. The campus which houses the garment factory school is highly inadequate; there is virtually no playground space. Another school has a 25 acre campus on rough terrain and has not had the funds to level off the ground. The school described above which started in a church lost its small playground when it constructed its new main building and then lost its parking lot when it constructed the gymnasium. One school is perched on top of a hill and the headmaster described it as, "One-half acre of campus and nine and one-half acres of hole." The hole is being filled with trash and fill dirt. This campus is especially unattractive—its small parking lot is "paved" with scraps of asphalt roofing material.

Inadequacies. A number of inadequacies of these schools have already been noted. There are others.

A principle inadequacy is the curriculum of the schools. None of the schools has enough teachers to provide real choices in a comprehensive curriculum. Even in the large school described above the teacher/pupil ratio was 34:1. That school did offer music and art which are absent in many schools, but required courses in religion, thereby further restricting choice. Although many of the schools claim general education as one of their goals, the only choices available outside the college preparatory curriculum are driver education, typing and additional mathematics courses. Most students take English, mathematics, history and science, plus one additional course. The full range of mathematics is offered in only a few schools and in others even the restricted range is made possible by alternating algebra I and plane geometry in successive years. Physics and chemistry are likewise alternated. In several instances a wider choice of classes was made possible by grouping students from grades 7 through 12. In most schools the range was less, but it was not uncommon to find at least three grades represented in one class.

The average number of teachers in the schools was 23 and the average number of pupils in a school was 465; thus, the average pupil/teacher ratio was about 20:1, a highly favorable ratio. Since, though, the schools, with one exception, had 12 grades and at least two sections were required for each grade 1 through 6, and the schools frequently had a kindergarten, the average school had only about 10 teachers for grades 7 through 12. These 10 teachers are needed in classrooms so that guidance counselors, librarians, and other special personnel are virtually absent. Several schools do not have a librarian and most have only a part-time librarian.

Four per cent of the teachers do not hold degrees and about 80 per cent hold only a bachelors degree and are frequently teaching in fields in which they have less than minimal preparation. About 17 per cent of the school personnel hold masters degrees and less than one per cent hold a sixth year degree or have completed two years of graduate study. These findings can be interpreted to mean that the teachers are poorly qualified when compared with teachers in the public schools.

Headmasters are also poorly qualified. The highest degree on one headmaster was the bachelor of divinity, another held only a bachelor of science degree. The remainder of the headmasters and principals held masters degrees, often in fields other than educational administration. One headmaster held the doctor of business administration. Only one school had both elementary and secondary principals; the remainder had only the headmaster, administrator or principal.

Twenty-one per cent of the teachers were in their first year of teaching and another 21 per cent had only one or two years of previous teaching experience. Twenty-two per cent had three to five years of experience. Thus, about two-thirds of the teachers had five years or less experience. These statistics are based on the report of the headmaster.

Twenty-one per cent of the teachers were less than 25 years of age, 26 per cent were between 25 and 30 years of age, 23 per cent between 31 and 35, 23 per cent between 36 and 50, and 7 per cent were above 50. Thus, in comparison with the public schools, the teaching faculty is young.

Only about 85 per cent of the teachers are certified or qualified to be certified as teachers in some state at the minimum level. The remainder are not qualified. Of the qualified teachers, many are teaching out of field.

The school libraries represented another area of weakness. In some schools there is no library or library books. In other schools the library is rudimentary and has no librarian. Only two schools had a full-time librarian. One school which has a part-time librarian two days each week uses female students as library aides. These aides are responsible for checking books in and out and for cleaning the library including the floor and windows. Only one school had an adequate library by Southern Association standards and this library was adequate only at the elementary level.

Audio-visual equipment is virtually absent. Elementary grades frequently have record players but equipment such as film strip projectors, movie projectors, overhead projectors, opaque projectors, tape recorders, portable TV recorders, language stations, and other basic equipment is practically non-existent. None of the schools had any automated learning equipment.

Furniture and other classroom and office equipment is inadequate old, and in poor condition. The best equipped room in each school invariably was the headmaster's office. Classrooms use old style one arm desks with inadequate writing surfaces. Much of the furniture has been purchased used or constructed by parents for the school. One school offers home economics. Its equipment consists of an electric stove (probably donated by a patron), a used refrigerator, cabinets constructed by a patron, a sink, and an electric sewing machine which had been donated by a garment factory. Unfortunately, as is the case with most commercial type sewing machines, the machine operates at too high a speed for the beginning students. Tables in art rooms are of local construction. Some schools have new furniture but this is rare. It was believed by one observer that the classroom furniture in one school had been donated by the local school system—markings on the seats would indicate this.

Testing efforts have been sporadic and a comprehensive program was present in only one elementary school where the principal was trained as a guidance counselor. In all other schools there was an absence of guidance personnel but the headmaster in one school had a degree in counseling and guidance, and was initiating a testing program during the current year. In other schools only a few tests have been given and in most schools the only data available resulted from college entrance examinations of one sort or another.

Health facilities are absent in all but one school. This school, the largest in the group, employs a school nurse who gives first aid and has a sick room. In this school all children who are taking medication leave the medicine with the nurse who is responsible for seeing that they follow correct schedules. Such a practice is frequent in the public schools. In most schools the only first aid assistance available was through the coach who was not always available and who had minimal, if any, preparation in the area.

Lockers exist in few of the schools. One school added lockers this year—its fifth in existence. Other schools make no provisions outside the homeroom for storing books, supplies, and outer garments. Lockers are a luxury which these schools cannot afford.

Supplies are limited. Some schools assess a supply fee as will be seen in a later section, and others assess a fee for special classes such as laboratory courses, driver education, and art. Most schools are reluctant to assess fees since tuition is so high, and attempt to provide supplies out of the tuition funds. As a result supplies are inadequate.

The care of buildings and grounds is frequently in the hands of the students since the schools cannot afford janitorial services. Three schools have janitorial services available and in only one of these is it adequate. Other schools have part time janitors or maids to sweep the floors and all other aspects of the school including dusting, washing of windows, cleaning of restrooms, etc. are given over to the students. In some schools there is no janitorial service. As can be imagined, these schools are dirty and unattractive. Few schools can afford the additional help needed to care for the campus. Most of the schools assign responsibility for care of school areas to particular classes.

Differences in Christian Schools and Academies. Two of the schools had the word Christian in their titles and a third claimed to be a Christian school and had a minister as the headmaster. However, in most instances it was difficult to tell the difference between a Christian school and an academy. Most of the academies say they are Christian which means to them that they maintain "the American way of life."

In one of the Christian schools, courses in religion and chapel attendance were required. In a second of the schools, courses in religion were available, and in the third the only religion which appeared in the school was a picture of Christ which was in the school library. One school claims a Christian philosophy of education but inquiry did not yield a clear definition of the meaning of the term.

On the other hand, religion is a strong factor in many of these schools. In one school not included in the project, teacher selection is based on religious beliefs; probably many others make similar demands. In that school teachers were required to tell the name of the church in which membership is held, the length of membership, the services attended regularly, if the person has assurance that he is a born-again Christian, to give the details of the salvation experience and tell if the spouse is converted. Applicants are asked to sign a doctrinal statement.

The application also sets out standards of conduct which include but are not limited to regularly witnessing their faith, exhibiting at all times a spirit of loyalty to the pastor, the administration of the church, the school, and fellow staff members, to wearing (for females) dresses not shorter than two inches above the floor when in an upright kneeling position (immodest clothing will not be tolerated), to strict adherence to the church's policy concerning separation from the world which includes no use of alcoholic beverages, no dancing, no movie attendance, abstention from foul language, conformance to the Scriptures in the company kept, no attendance of secret societies, no use of tobacco in any form, and others.

None of the 11 schools included in the study was religious to the extent shown by the above school and it is not the impression of the study group that most schools with the name Christian differ to any great extent from those with the name Academy. Actually, one school with the name Academy had a stronger religious emphasis than the two schools with the name Christian.

Transportation. In all schools but one, the school has nothing to do with the transportation. In fact, in two schools the headmaster makes a point of not being outside the school when the children are arriving or leaving so that he does not become involved in any responsibility for supervising transportation.

A basic form of transportation is car pooling. Some children drive their own automobiles but, generally speaking, these students do not own or drive automobiles to school. In one school where there are more student drivers than in the average school, supervision of the student parking area is delegated to the senior class.

Some form of bus transportation is available in most of the schools. Most frequently, parents in a geographical area group together, charge subscription fees and a monthly transportation charge, and either rent bus service or purchase their own bus and employ a driver. In any event, the school has no responsibility for transportation.

In one school, there is a fleet of school-owned buses which operate on fixed routes and for which a monthly transportation fee is charged. Until the year of the study, these buses had been painted in the school's colors—red and white. Last year the state legislature decreed that all school buses must be painted international orange which was a financial problem for the school.

Missions of the Schools. Each headmaster was asked to describe the mission of his school. In most instances these descriptions repeated what advertising brochures said. In other instances there were interesting deviations. In general, the mission of the school is described significantly different from the descriptions given by parents as will be seen in a later section.

The following are direct quotations of responses to the question, "What is the mission of your school?" 1. Provide a good college preparation and a general education for those not planning to attend college (this school offers few options in its high school curriculum; the *Faculty Handbook* cites the purpose as, "The primary function of the school is to promote the understanding, maintenance (*sic.*), and improvement of the American way of life."); 2. College preparation, vocational preparation, general education (but few choices are available in the curriculum); 3. College preparation; 4. College preparation and vocational (only vocational course available is typewriting); 5. College prep for minority, general education; 6. College prep; 7. College prep; 8. Best preparation possible for post high school education (In a school where less than 30 per cent of the children will attend any post high school institution); 9. General education 10. College prep; 11. College preparation, general education, all subject matter taught from a Christian Philosophy.

In another section of the information schedule the headmaster was asked to describe the reasons for forming the school. These

---

QUESTIONNAIRE A

HEADMASTER QUESTIONNAIRE

Dear Headmaster:

Your cooperation in providing the information requested on the following pages will be most helpful to us in understanding the school, its mission, its means of support, and other important considerations. Your help is very much appreciated.

1. What do you consider to be the mission of your school (for example, college preparation, vocational preparation, general education, etc.)?

2. Number of teachers in your school:

3. a. How many of your teachers do not hold degrees?
   b. How many of your teachers hold the bachelor's degree?
   c. How many of your teachers hold the master's degree:
   d. How many of your teachers hold an EdS degree or are certified by some state at the sixth year level?
   e. How many of your teachers hold the doctorate?

4. How many of your teachers are certified or are eligible to be certified to teach in some state?

Instruments are from R.E. Bills, *A System for Assessing Affectivity*, University: The University of Alabama Press, 1975.

---

elicited responses which are interesting when compared to the above statements of mission. Again quoting from the headmasters, they said: 1. To provide a better school and to escape the problems of mass integration; 2. To extend church influence; 3. Quality of education, desire to maintain standards above national average (records show they have not achieved this); 4. To meet needs of students; 5. To avoid attendance at city high school located 45 minutes to one hour away by public transportation after area zoned (for integration); 6. Poorest operated public school system in the state, achievement four years below national norm; 7. To give the student of the community a chance for a high quality education (This statement was made regarding what is probably the poorest school of the group of 11); 8. Integration and a declining level of public education; 9. To create an environment for quality education, to serve as a standard setting institution, and to foster Christian faith in policy, practices and persons (This school makes no claim to be a Christian school.); 10. To provide education with Christian philosophy and principles.

Building and Constructions Costs. The headmasters provided

Questionnaire A, Continued

5. How many of your teachers have had less than one year of teaching experience (excluding this year)?
   One or two years of previous teaching experience?
   Three to five years of experience?
   Six to ten years of experience?
   More than ten years of experience?

6. How many of your teachers fall in each of the following groups?
   less than 25 years of age
   25 to 30 years of age
   31 to 35 years of age
   36 to 50 years of age
   Above 50 years of age

7. Degrees held by principals:
   a. Elementary
   b. Junior High or Middle School
   c. High School
   d. Headmaster

8. Please check to describe your organizational plan:
   6-3-3
   8-4
   4-4-4
   Other

---

information regarding constructions funds for the original and/or additional buildings. These included: 1. Selling memberships; 2. Tuition and bonds; 3. Loans and donations; 4. Fund raising and tuition; 5. Bond issue plus construction fee; 6. Loan secured by a 25 year mortgage (it is doubtful that this building will last this long); 7. Building was donated; 8. Purchased used building; 9. Paid for out of operating funds creating a $60,000 debt and organizing a drive to pay it off; 10. Direct solicitation; 11. Donations and bond program.

Purchase of Equipment. Funds for purchase of equipment were obtained from a variety of sources. In general where equipment was paid for from tuition, it was most inadequate. Audio-visual equipment is the least adequate equipment in the schools and is, for all practical purposes, absent. Classroom furniture and office equipment, as noted earlier, is old and inadequate. According to the headmaster the equipment was obtained by: 1. Selling memberships; 2. Bonds and tuition;. 3. Fund raising and tuition; 4. Bond issues, donations, and a construction fee; 5. Tuition; 6. Tuition and dona-

---

Questionnaire A, Continued

9. What is the charge for tuition and fees per student?

10. Is your school affiliated with another institution such as a church or other? (please check correct response)   □   no □ If yes, what is the other institution?

11. If your school is affiliated with another institution, what is the nature of the affiliation?
   a. We are a part of the other institution: yes □   no □
   b. We receive financial support from the other institution: yes □   no □
   c. We are accountable to the other institution: yes □   no □
   d. We receive *only* encouragement from the other institution: yes □ no □
   Comments

12. Are you, as headmaster, responsible to a board? yes □   no □
   If yes, please describe the nature of the relationship:

13. If you have a board, how are its members choosen?

14. Do you pay state and local property taxes on your buildings? yes □   no □
   Equipment? yes □   no □ Real estate: yes □   no □ Other?
   yes □   no □

15. In addition to tuition do the children pay fees for any classes? yes □   no □
   If yes, for what classes?

---

tions plus magazine sales; 7. Donations and tuition; 8. Tuition and donations.

Nine schools reported that they purchased at least some equipment and furniture new, six purchased used furniture, one had furniture donated by a school system (this may not have been illegal since the furniture had outlived its usefulness), seven schools constructed some of their own furniture, and three systems purchased used furniture from other schools. The headmasters rated their furniture as: 1. adequate; 2. average; 3. poor; 4. good; 5. poor; 6. inadequate; 7. poor; 8. poor; 9. average; 10. poor; 11. good.

Sources of funds for purchase of audio-visual equipment were given as: gifts—local clubs and organizations, library fee, general fund, parent teacher organization and candy sales, budget and gifts, tuition, and tuition and gifts. They rated their audio-visual equipment as: fair—not enough, poor, poor, fair, inadequate, poor, inadequate, inadequate, fair, inadequate.

Tuition and Fees. Tuition and fees vary considerably from school to school Listed below are the various arrangements.

Questionnaire A, Continued

16. How are the children transported to school?

17. If private buses or buses owned by the school are used, what is the monthly charge per student?

18. Do you receive any *direct* financial support for your school from any public source? yes ☐   no ☐ Please comment, if yes:

19. Do you receive any *indirect* financial support for your school from any public source? yes ☐   no ☐ Please comment:

20. Is your school accredited? yes ☐   no ☐ If yes, what is the name of the accrediting group

21. In what year did you add the last grade to your school?
    Number of grades in your school at present

22. What were the reasons for forming the school?

23. If available, please give total enrollments by year:
    1974-75   1969-70
    1973-74   1968-69
    1972-73   1967-68
    1971-72   1966-67
    1970-71   1965-66

---

1. $600 membership fee per family. Tuition per month $50 one child, $80 two children, $100 three or more children. Books $15 grades 7-12, $10 grades 1-6. Supplies $5 per child. Driver education $20, home economics $40, typing $20, art $10, mechanical drawing $10. Memberships purchased by churches and non parents assigned as scholarships on an annual basis. Memberships depreciate at the rate of 30% per year. Buses (private): initiation fee plus $10 per month.
2. Tuition: K-8 $55 per month, 9-12 $57.50 per month. Driver education, typing, physical education, and library fees of unstated amount. (Church school)
3. Tuition: First child in family $475, second and third $400 each, no additional charge for more than three. Pre-school $250. Initiation fee per family $1500. Unstated activity fee. Private buses $12 to $15 per month.
4. Tuition: $830. Fees for typing, art, science, testing, and transportation $110 per child per year. (Total cost per child per year $940.)

Questionnaire A, Continued

24. Check *each* of the following which apply: How would you describe the teaching methodologies in your school:
    Traditional
    Progressive
    Self contained classes
    Team teaching
    Differentiated staffing
    Open classroom
    Ungraded
    Departmentalized
    Resources teachers combined with self-contained classrooms
    Homogeneous grouping
    Heterogeneous grouping
    Other
    Please comment

25. Is your scheduling of classes traditional   or otherwise
    Please comment

26. Are consultative services for improving your school available to you: yes ☐ no ☐   If consultative services are available for a fee, can the school afford the charges? yes ☐   no ☐ Please comment

---

5. Tuition: $55 per month. Typing fee $25. Building construction fee.

6. Tuition: high school $800, elementary school $700. Typing fee $50. Building fee $600 per family.

7. $100 non-refundable registration fee. Tuition: K-6 $600, 7-12 $750. Instructional fees $35 per child.

8. Family membership $300. Tuition: 1-7 $450, 8-12 $500. $20 per year book rental fee.

9. Application fee: $100 per family. Tuition: 1 child $650, 2 children $1100, 3 children $1450, 4 children $1650, 5 children $1800, 6 children $1950, $100 per child over 6 in family. Annual membership fee $25 per family. Books and supplies $25 per child per year. Admission tests: new student $10 per child, all students $5. Fees: typing $18, driver education $25, science $10. Private buses, costs vary from bus to bus.

10. Tuition: grade 1 $680, 2-4 $715, 5-8 $790, 9-12 $850. Optional: Baldridge Reading and Study Skills Program. Private bus

---

Questionnaire A, Continued

27. Please estimate how much money the average parent pays for books and materials for a child at each of the following levels:
    grades
    1-3 $
    4-6 $
    7-9 $
    10-12 $

28. What is the average age of your elementary school textbooks?
    Junior High
    High School

29. Please describe where your students come from (for example, "They all live within one-half mile of the school")

30. What sources of financial support does your school have other that tuition and fees?

31. What interschool athletics does your school participate in?

32. Please list the extracurricular activities of your school

33. How does the school select its textbooks?

---

transportation: $125 initiation fee, 1 child $20 per month, each additional child $5 per month.

11. Tuition: $550. Private bus fees $20 per month.

Textbooks. Ten of the 11 schools purchase their textbooks new and one purchases used textbooks. In some instances the book charge is included in the tuition and in other cases there is an extra charge for the books. In a few instances the children can purchase textbooks from a local bookstore. The headmasters listed the following arrangements: rent to students, rent to students, loan, purchase by student from school or other source, purchase by student from school or other source, rent at beginning of year sometimes sell at end of year, school supplies as part of tuition, loaned to students, school provides.

Costs for books and materials average about $25 per child per year. The average age of the books the schools own is about three years. This age probably will increase as the schools become older.

Textbooks usually are selected by the faculty but in one instance

---

Questionnaire A, Continued

34. What is the source of your textbooks:
    Purchased new: yes ☐   no ☐
    Purchased secondhand: yes ☐   no ☐
    Purchased from some public school system: yes ☐   no ☐
    Other

35. Do you see students' textbooks or do they purchase them from some other source?

36. How would you describe the adequacy of your audio-visual equipment?

37. What is the source of support for your audio-visual equipment?

38. Does your school have a hot lunch program at noon? yes ☐   no ☐
    Do you serve breakfast? yes ☐   no ☐

39. How would you describe the age and condition of your office and classroom furniture?

---

the headmaster uses the textbooks approved by another Christian school.

Other Sources of Financial Support. A variety of other means of support are available to the schools. The headmasters listed the following: athletics, advertisements in yearbooks and programs, parent teacher organization projects; none; horse show, fall festival, donations, fund raising, sale of peanuts and candy, raffles, athletics, school paper, testing fees; Title I and II, gifts and fund raising, donations and projects or drives; gifts, athletics, carnivals, fund raising of students and parents; contributions from parents and friends, church donations; magazine sales.

Organization. There are almost as many plans of organization as there are schools. Three schools list a 6-3-3 organization and others list 2-7-5, 8-12, 1-6 and 7-12, 1-7 and 8-12, 4-3-5, 6-3-4, 5-4-3, and 1-9 and 10-12. A primary factor in the organization for most of the schools is the arrangement of buildings and locations of buildings. In other words, the organizational plans seldom reflect a philosophy of education but are dictated by the available space.

Within the plan of organization, teaching strategies show little variety. Nine of the schools described themselves as traditional and two believed they were progressive. All of the schools have self-contained classrooms in the lower grades and departmentalization starting at the junior high school level or high school level except for one school which claims departmentalization in grade five. None

---

Questionnaire A, Continued

40. What was the source of your classroom furniture (please answer all that are applicable):
    Purchased new: yes ☐   no ☐
    Purchased used: yes ☐   no ☐
    Donated by a school system: yes ☐   no ☐
    We constructed some of it: yes ☐   no ☐
    Purchased used from some school system: yes ☐   no ☐
    Other:

41. How was the money raised to build your building(s)?

42. How was the money raised to equip your building(s)?

---

of the schools use homogeneous grouping as far as could be determined but two schools claim to use it.

In 10 of the 11 schools, scheduling of classes is traditional. In the remaining school, all classes rotate on a regular schedule with the exception of the sixth, and last, period.

Institutional Affiliations. Of the 11 schools only two had institutional affiliations. In the first of these the school uses part of the church property and has built two additional buildings on the church grounds. In the second, the school is sponsored by a church.

Control. Each of the schools has a board of control but in each the relationship varies. In ten of the schools the headmaster or administrator is responsible to the board but in the other school the headmaster is responsible only to the chairman of the board. Responsibilities of the headmaster differ from school to school; in some instances he functions as a superintendent and recommends policy to the board, the employment of personnel, and the items in the budget. In other instances the headmaster serves only to execute the board's orders and does not administer the school—the school is administered by the board.

There is also much variety in the manner in which the board is formed. Arrangements include: election of the board members by the parents, selection of the board members by the church deacons, a self perpetuating board which elects its own successors, a permanent board, a board elected by the foundation members, election to the board by the board after recommendations by the parents, and nomination by the board and election by the parent teacher organization.

Taxes. None of these schools pay local or state property taxes on buildings, equipment, or real estate. They state that they pay no taxes of any form except one school pointed out that it paid gasoline taxes for its one school bus which is used to transport athletic teams.

In spite of the form of public support provided by their tax exempt status, 10 of the 11 schools stated that they receive no direct or indirect financial support from any public source. The one exception was the school which has signed the compliance statement required by the Civil Rights Act and which recognizes that it receives both direct and indirect financial support from public sources.

Accreditation. Only one of the schools was in any manner accredited by a regional or state accreditation agency other than those of their own organization. The newly developed schools in each of the seven states included in the area covered by this study have formed their own state associations which, in turn, accredits the schools. Standards of these associations are far inferior to those of state and regional accrediting agencies which serve the public schools.

In one instance the accreditation team of the state association is headed by a dean of the education college in a state university and visiting teams usually include at least one or two members of the faculty.

Consultative services are not available to these schools because of the lack of funds for this purpose and the only help available for improvement work is through the voluntary work of faculty members in institutions of higher education. All public schools have such consultative services freely available through their state universities and colleges.

The one exception noted above was in the case of a 12 grade school which had its elementary grades approved by the Southern Association of Colleges and Schools and which is going to apply in the near future for approval of its high school by SACS.

Athletics. Although the schools profess to see themselves primarily as college preparatory institutions, each forms athletic teams soon after the school is organized. It is an interesting phenomenon to observe that parents who frequently decry the emphasis on athletics in the public schools makes provisions for football fields and gymnasia for inter-school basketball along with provisions for classrooms. It is quite possible that along with other reasons, the parents make such provisions for their own satisfaction and to keep their children from feeling deprived. A principle reason for forming state associations is to provide athletic conferences in which the school teams can participate. Representatives of the schools to the association meetings usually include the head coach.

Eight of the schools have football teams, ten have basketball, five have track and golf, six have baseball, four have tennis, and two have soccer. Football is the sport which is most likely to exploit the boys. Schools field football teams even if there are insufficient numbers of boys to produce a winning team and use players who are undersized by any standard in inter-school competition. When one of the team members asked a coach about the problem of his under-size boys, he responded, "It will make men of them and they are growing rapidly."

Enrollments. Generalizations regarding enrollment trends are difficult to make. If there are trends present they are in the direction of rapid growth in the years immediately following formation of the school and a leveling off or decline in subsequent years. Leveling off probably occurs if the school is acceptable to the parents and if the pool of prospective students is heavily drawn upon. Declines occur when parents become disillusioned.

It is interesting to note that these schools do not escape all of the problems which face public schools. In one instance during the year of the study, one school was approached by a school in a small community ten miles away and asked to merge (consolidate is the term used in the public schools). After a long period of bargaining the larger school (the one in the study) agreed to merge and presented what appeared to be fair terms for the merger. At this point a group of residents in the small community who were not patrons of the school objected and obtained a court injunction to halt the merger. The objection was based on the claim that property values would decline if the school were to be moved to another town. After the hearing the injunction was dissolved and the schools will merge.

Listed below are the enrollments of 10 of the 11 schools for the period 1965-66 to 1974-75.

See School Enrollments Table on following page.

SCHOOL ENROLLMENTS

School	1974-75	1973-74	1972-73	1971-72	1970-71	1969-70	1968-69	1967-68	1966-67
1	548	535	500	464	468				
2	637	630	575	480	700				
3	292	240	180	175	230	170	100		
4	1,135	1,150	1,300	700	500	150			
5	130	125	119	75					
6	255	210	206	200	160	120*			
7	258	249	247	222	225				
8	552	570							
9	226	252	268	240	240	203	252	211	164**
10	620	624	494	264					

Notes:

*This school is credited in the text of this report with 240 students for 1974-75 since the enrollment included that number at the time of testing.
This school occupies the garment factory building. Enrollments do not include the period when the school occupied the residence.

**Enrollment for this school for 1965-66 was 11 students.

School No. 5 includes Grades 8-12 only.

3

Attitudes Toward Schools

Each school was visited and a variety of instruments was administered to determine more about the affective learning of the students and the climate for affective learning in the school. The data for each school were examined and an individual report was written for each school which included suggestions for improvement of the school. The data for the entire group of schools were analyzed with the results which are reported below.

QUESTIONNAIRE B

PARENT QUESTIONNAIRE

Dear Parents:

We want to know how you see our school so we would appreciate your taking a few minutes to answer the questions on the following pages. Wherever possible we would appreciate having responses from both parents working together. You will not be asked to identify yourself on the answer sheet and your responses will be kept confidential. **Please do not give your name or any other identifying information on the answer sheet.**

If you have only one child in this school, you are asked to fill out only one answer sheet. If you have more than one child in the school, but they are all in *one* of the following grade groups, you will still only fill out one answer sheet: grades 1-3, 4-6, 7-9, 10-12. If you have a child in more than one of these grade groups, please fill out an answer sheet for each grade group in which you have a child.

On the first testing day each student in grades 1-12 was asked to take home a copy of the Parent Inventory and to return it the following day. In most instances all copies of the inventory were not returned the following day and late returns were mailed to the project team.

The Parent Inventory usually consists of 35 items; however, the instrument was modified for this study to provide 40 items of information. A copy of the modified instrument appears as Questionnaire B and on it are noted the responses of the total parent group. This group consists of 2,976 parent groups (both parents were asked to work together in responding).

In addition to item responses, the Parent Inventory can be scored to give a measure of the positiveness of the parents' attitudes toward the schools. The average score of the 2,976 parents in the 11 private schools was 13.8 and scores ranged from a low of -25 (a parent set which felt negatively about their school) to a high of 35. The average of 13.8 may be compared with the average score on this instrument for public school parents of 10.1. This comparison shows

---

Questionnaire B, Continued

To answer, please use the answer sheet. *Please do not roll or crumple the answer sheet and ask your child to be as careful with it as possible.* Make your marks on the answer sheet with **a soft lead pencil with black lead**, and make your marks as heavy as possible. Please blacken the entire space between the brackets to indicate your answer, being as careful as possible and making no "stray" marks. If you make a stray mark or if you wish to change an answer, please erase carefully and fully. **Mark only one choice for each item.**

Please be careful that you use the correct item number on the answer sheet in answering the questions. These are the numbers which go from 1 through 160. Incidentally, this answer sheet is used for a good many different purposes so you will not need to use all 160 items. Since there are only 40 questions on this inventory, you will use only items 1 through 40. Also, please notice that the numbers go across the page and not down each column as you might expect.

Likewise, you do not have to complete the blanks on the side of the page or answer anything in the blocks at the top of the page. Your responses will be kept confidential and no effort will be made to identify you.

Your time and trouble will help us build a better school for your children. Please let us know exactly how you feel. **The return of this sheet and the completed answer sheets tomorrow or at your earliest convenience will be appreciated.**

Sincerely,

The Faculty and Administration

---

that the average parent feels more positively about the private schools than the average public school parent feels about his school.

As noted earlier in the report, the more positive attitudes of the parents of the private schools is probably the result of several factors. These parents believe that private schools are automatically superior to public schools—they must believe this to make the effort and the expense worthwhile. Second, there is always pride of ownership and this affects attitude. But most importantly, these schools are highly responsive to the wishes and desires of these parents. They must have the financial support of the parents. Too, the parents are more continuously in contact with the schools than are the parents of public school children. The private schools are usually located closer to the parents' homes than are the public schools. The public schools provide transportation so that parents visit them only infrequently. In contrast, the private school parents have opportunity for as much as two or more contacts per day with the schools.

But the more positive average noted above is not true for all of the private schools. The school averages ranged from a low of 8.3 to

---

Questionnaire B, Continued

1. The number of children we have in this school is:
   1. one. (1210—*40.7%*)
   2. two. (1169—*39.3%*)
   3. three. (471—*15.8%*)
   4. four. (91—*3.1%*)
   5. five or more. (23—*0.8%*)
      12 parents or 0.4% did not respond

2. We are answering *this* questionnaire for our child or children in grade group:
   1. 1, 2, or 3. (672—*22.6%*)
   2. 4, 5, or 6. (797—*26.8%*)
   3. 7, 8, or 9. (910—*30.6%*)
   4. 10, 11, or 12. (576—*19.4%*)
      21 or 0.7% did not respond

3. Our child's father went to school as follows:
   1. he did not complete elementary school (six years of school. (28—*0.9%*
   2. he completed elementary school. (196—*6.6%*)
   3. he completed secondary school (grades six through eleven or twelve). (1880—*63.2%*)
   4. he completed college. (531—*17.8%*)
   5. he did graduate study. (317—*10.7%*)
      24 or 0.8% did not respond

---

a high of 18.1. The garment factory school had the lowest average and a school located in a rural area, and more distant from the childrens' homes than the average school in the study, was next to lowest. On the other hand, three of the five highest schools were the Christian schools. Statistical examination of the parents' attitudes in the 11 schools showed that highly significant differences existed among the averages for the schools. Thus, although on the average the parents of the children in the 11 schools feel more positively toward their schools than the average public school parent, the private school parents also vary considerably among each other in their attitudes toward the schools. Positive parent attitudes are not an automatic concomitant of their children's attendance at a private school.

Data for public schools have been examined by grade level and it has been noted that parent attitudes vary significantly with the grade placement of their children. The same is true for the data of this study. Parents of children in grades 1-3 had an average attitude score of 13.1, for grades 4-6 the average was 11.3, for grades 7-9 it

---

Questionnarie B, Continued

4. Our child's mother went to school as follows:
   1. she did not complete elementary school. (9—0.3%)
   2. she completed elementary school. (124—4.2%)
   3. she completed secondary school. (2161—72.6%)
   4. she completed college. (449—16.8%)
   5. she did graduate study. (162—5.4%)
      21 or 0.7% no response

5. In general, we feel that the school is:
   1. a very good school. (992—33.3%)
   2. a good school. (1341—45.1%)
   3. an average school. (554—18.6%)
   4. a poor school. (42—1.4%)
   5. we have no opinion. (33—1.1%)
      14 or 0.5% no response

6. In general, we feel that teachers and other school officials in treating our child:
   1. are always fair. (745—25.0%)
   2. are usually fair. (1828—61.4%)
   3. are sometimes unfair. (299—10.0%)
   4. are often unfair. (37—1.2%)
   5. we have no opinion. (55—1.8%)
      12 or 0.4% no response

---

was 9.0, and for grades 10-12 it was 8.9. Thus, the higher the grade level of the child in these private schools, the less positively the parents feel about the school. It must be noted, however, that the decline from grade level to grade level in these private schools is not nearly so great as for the public schools; at all levels the private school average was above that of the comparable public school average.

These responses present some interesting information. Items #3 and #4 shows that as in the public schools, mothers have a higher level of education than fathers. In contrast to the public school parents, though, it is observed that the educational level of the group is high. A survey of a large public school system made during the same period as this study showed that in the public school system 53.8 per cent of the fathers and 61.4 per cent of the mothers were high school graduates.

The responses to item #5 give an overall impression of the parents' attitudes toward their schools. More than 78 per cent believe their school is either a very good school or a good school. The low

---

Questionnaire B, Continued

7. In general, we feel that the teachers and other school officials in dealing with our child are:
   1. not firm enough. (419—*14.1%*)
   2. about as firm as they should be. (2346—*78.8%*)
   3. too firm. (54—*1.8%*)
   4. We have no opinion. (134—*4.5%*)
      23 or 0.8% no response

8. Of the following, we believe it is *most* important for the school to:
   1. help children decide whether or not to go to college. (84—*2.8%*)
   2. help children acquire good manners, poise, personal appearance, and self confidence. (187—*6.3%*)
   3. help children discover their vocational interests and abilities. (1196—*40.2%*)
   4. help children develop work habits and study skills. (1471—*49.4%*)
   5. help pupils learn to control their conduct. (13—*0.4%*)
      No response 25 or 0.8%

9. In regard to the answer we gave question #8, we believe that:
   1. the school is doing a poor job. (87—*2.9%*)
   2. the job the school is doing needs to be improved. (1065—*35.8%*)
   3. the school is doing a good job. (1550—*52.1%*)
   4. we have no opinion. (225—*7.6%*)
      No response 49 or 1.6%

---

percentage of no opinion and no response to this item is worthy of special note. When compared to the responses of many of the more important items, it is found that parents have or are willing to state an opinion to this item but do not respond as freely to the more important items. In fact, the pattern of no opinion and no response answers suggests that many of these parents either do not have opinions on important items or are fearful of stating them if they are in disagreement with the majority opinion. The latter is probably correct, for some parents indicated they would not respond to the inventory since they thought the school might make an attempt to determine what they said.

Responses to items #6 and #7 and similar items account for the higher average attitude of the parents of children in these schools. More than 86 per cent of the parents believe that the teachers and other school officials are always or usually fair in treating their children and almost 79 per cent believe that teachers and other school officials are as firm as they should be in treating their children. Responses to these two items also illustrate another dif-

---

Questionnaire B, Continued

10. Of the following, we believe it is *most* important for the school to help pupils learn:
    1. to distinguish right from wrong and to guide their actions accordingly. (**1326**—*44.6%*)
    2. to get along with other people. (**271**—*9.1%*)
    3. a set of moral values. (**365**—*12.3%*)
    4. courtesy and obedience. (**136**—*4.6%*)
    5. to solve their problems for themselves. (**836**—*28.1%*)
         No response 42 or 1.4%

11. In regard to the answer we gave question #10, we believe that:
    1. the school is doing a poor job. (**94**—*3.2%*)
    2. the job the school is doing needs to be improved. (**870**—*29.2%*)
    3. the school is doing a good job. (**1659**—*55.7%*)
    4. We have no opinion. (**276**—*9.3%*)
         No response 77 or 2.6%

12. Of the following, we believe it is *most* important for the school to:
    1. stress the teaching of the basic school subjects. (**855**—*28.7%*)
    2. help pupils learn to think for themselves. (**632**—*21.2%*)
    3. help pupils learn how to study. (**453**—*15.2%*)
    4. help pupils learn how to take independent action. (**132**—*4.4%*)
    5. help pupils choose and prepare for their life work. (**878**—*29.5%*)
         No response 26 or 0.9%

---

ference between this group of parents and those of public school children. The parents in these private schools are much more homogeneous in their opinions than are the public school parents.

Item #8 is an exception to the above generalization. The parents showed a difference of opinion in what is most important for the school to do for children. Forty per cent believe the school should help children discover their vocational interests and abilities and more than 49 per cent believe the school should help the children develop work habits and study skills. Since, though, responses are concentrated on these two alternatives, a higher degree of homogeneity of response is shown by these parents than those in the public schools.

Although, in respect to responses to item #9, 52 per cent of the parents believe the school is doing a good job of the goal they selected in item #8, almost 36 per cent stated that the job the school is doing needs to be improved.

In item #10, about 45 per cent of the parents stated that the most important thing the schools could do would be to help pupils learn to

---

Questionnaire B, Continued

13. In regard to the answer we gave question #12, we believe that:
    1. the school is doing a poor job. (109—3.7%)
    2. the job the school is doing needs to be improved. (1030—34.6%)
    3. the school is doing a good job. (1540—51.7%)
    4. we have no opinion. (240—8.1%)
       No response 57 or 1.9%

14. In regard to the help which teachers give our child on his homework:
    1. they give him all the help he needs. (1301—43.7%)
    2. more help is needed. (1086—36.5%)
    3. much more help is needed. (263—8.8%)
    4. we have no opinion. (270—9.1%)
       No response 56 or 1.9%

15. In general, the amount of homework which the teachers require is:
    1. entirely too much. (253—8.5%)
    2. about as it should be. (2260—75.9%)
    3. too little. (323—10.9%)
    4. we have no opinion. (103—3.5%)
       No response 37 or 1.2%

---

distinguish right from wrong and to guide their actions accordingly. The second most important goal was selected by 28 per cent of the group and stated that the school should help pupils learn to solve their problems for themselves. Again, there is considerable agreement among the parents.

The responses to item #11 suggest some disagreement in the success the schools are having in securing the goals selected by the parents. Almost 56 per cent believe the school is doing a good job but 29 per cent believe the job needs improving. The similarity of the percentages in items #11 and #10 suggests that those parents who want the school to help pupils learn to distinguish right from wrong and to guide their actions accordingly are possibly more satisfied with the job the school is doing than those who selected problem solving as the goal.

Item #12 shows considerable disagreement among the parents. The highest percentage selecting a goal was about 30 and this goal was to help pupils choose and prepare for their life work. The next most important goals, in decreasing order, were stress the teaching of

---

Questionnaire B, Continued

16. The annual income of our family is:
    1. less than $6,000. (71—2.4%)
    2. $6,000 to $9,000 (234—7.9%)
    3. more than $9,000 but less than $12,000. (381—12.8%)
    4. more than $12,000 but less than $15,000. (616—20.7%)
    5. more than $15,000. (1480—49.7%)
       No response 194 or 6.5%

17. In regard to help in solving personal problems, we believe the school:
    1. offers enough help. (596—20.0%)
    2. should provide more help. (293—9.8%)
    3. we don't know how much help is provided. (1704—57.3%)
    4. we don't think the school should offer help with personal problems. (145—4.9%)
    5. we have no opinion. (213—7.2%)
       No response 25 or 0.8%

18. In respect to social problems, we believe the school:
    1. offers enough help. (619—20.8%)
    2. should provide more help. (283—9.5%)
    3. we don't know how much help is provided. (1681—56.5%)
    4. we don't think the school should offer help with social problems. (121—4.1%)
    5. we have no opinion. (244—8.2%)
       No response 28 or 0.9%

---

the basic school subjects, help pupils learn to think for themselves, and help pupils learn how to study. As shown by responses to item #13 there was less satisfaction with the achievement of the school in this area than in the area described by item #8 and that described by item #10.

An even more interesting conclusion can be inferred from the responses to items #8, #10, and #12 than that which is shown by their manifest content.

First, however, it is useful to point out that there are at least three levels of morality shown by people. These have been called preconventional, conventional, and principled. In preconventional morality the person responds in terms of "What's in it for me" meaning sometimes that he responds in terms of the rewards or punishments he will receive in the general sense of "you scratch my back and I'll scratch yours" or "if you do this for me, I will do that for you." At the conventional level, the person responds in terms of a set of "absolutes" or a set of moral values which usually has not grown from personal experience but has been imposed from outside by the home, the

---

Questionnaire B, Continued

19. In general, the help provided our child is choosing the courses he should take:
    1. is sufficient. (878—29.5%)
    2. should be increased. (539—18.1%)
    3. we don't know how much help is provided. (577—19.4%)
    4. help is not needed at this school level. (760—25.5%)
    5. we have no opinion. (187—6.3%
       No response 35 or 1.2%

20. In general, the discipline in school is:
    1. too stern. (58—1.9%)
    2. too varied from teacher to teacher. (817—27.5%)
    3. satisfactory. (1610—54.1%)
    4. not strict enough. (363—12.2)
    5. we have no opinion. (101—3.4%)
       No response 27 or 0.9%

21. We feel that the opening hour of school is:
    1. too early. (58—1.9%)
    2. too late. (85—2.9%)
    3. about correct. (2784—93.5
    4. we have no opinion. (19—0.6%)
       No response 30 or 1.0%

---

church, or otherwise. At the conventional level, since the values never really become the person's and since it is difficult to find absolutes, the person will be more inconsistent in his behavior from situation to situation and also more anxious because he is never certain that other people will approve of his behavior or that he has done the "right" thing. At the principled level, the person's values have grown from his own experience; they are a part of him and it becomes easier for him to decide how he should behave. He is more concerned with acting in a manner consistent with his own beliefs than in pleasing other people.

The three levels of morality differ from each other along a concrete-abstract continuum. At the pre-conventional level the person's concerns are related to concretes. For example, at the junction between pre-conventional and conventional, if the person is a member of a church, it probably will be one described as fundamental and in it sin has a highly concrete character. Manner of dress, hair style, jewelry, and other such concerns may characterize the individual's thinking. At the conventional level there is likewise a

---

Questionnaire B, Continued

22. We feel that the lunch hour of the school is:
    1. too short. (**368**—*12.4%*)
    2. about correct. (**2280**—*76.6%*)
    3. too long. (**37**—*1.2%*)
    4. we have no opinion. (239—*8.0%*)
        No response 52 or 1.8%

23. We feel that the information which the school provides us about our child's progress is:
    1. sufficient. (**2133**—*71.7%*)
    2. insufficient. (**742**—*24.9%*)
    3. we have no opinion. (**69**—*2.3%*)
        No response 32 or 1.1%

24. We feel that pupil activities (clubs, school parties, athletics, etc.):
    1. are very valuable. (**1060**—*35.6%*)
    2. are valuable. (**1685**—*56.6%*)
    3. subtract from the value of the school program. (**78**—*2.6%*)
    4. have no place in a school. (**12**—*0.4%*)
    5. we have no opinion. (**112**—*3.8%*)
        No response 29 or 1.0%

---

concrete aspect to the person's concerns but when these are examined it is found that he is attempting to make that which is relative become absolute. Traits such as honesty, truthfulness, sincerity are seen to exist in an absolute form and supposedly are sought as ends in themselves. At the principled level, thought and guidelines are abstract. Indeed, those principles which guide the person's morality have been *abstracted* from his experience and are seen as guides or ideals not as absolutes.

The parents' responses to items #8, #10, and #12 show clearly that the majority of the parents exist at a conventional level of morality; some are at the pre-conventional level and others at the principled level. This finding echoes what was already known— these parents have absolute standards of right and wrong and the formation of their schools is a means by which they seek to do that which they firmly believe to be right. As will be seen, the children in these schools are likewise very much at the conventional level of morality.

Although a large proportion of the parents feel that the schools

---

Questionnaire B, Continued

25. The distance we live from school is:
    1. one-half mile or less. (**211**—*7.1%*)
    2. more than one-half mile but not more than one mile. (**165**—*5.5%*)
    3. more than one mile but less than two miles. (**234**—*7.9%*)
    4. more than two miles but less than five miles. (**513**—*17.2%*)
    5. five miles or more. (**1821**—*61.2%*)
       No response 32 or 1.1%

26. We feel that the school year is:
    1. too long. (**86**—*2.9%*)
    2. too short. (**55**—*1.8%*)
    3. about right. (**2770**—*93.1%*)
    4. we have no opinion. (**39**—*1.3%*)
       No response 26 or 0.8%

27. In regard to the subjects which are taught, we feel that:
    1. the school tries to offer too much. (**23**—*0.8%*)
    2. offerings should be limited more to the "basic" subjects. (**145**—*4.9%*)
    3. there is not enough choice. (**518**—*17.4%*)
    4. in general, they are about right. (**2076**—*69.8%*)
    5. we have no opinion. (**193**—*6.5%*)
       No response 21 or 0.7%

---

give their children all the help they need their homework (item #13), over one-third believe more help is needed.

About half of the families reported annual incomes of more than $15,000. This appears to be higher than would be expected and the impressions of the headmasters with whom the matter was checked was that it was too high. On further reflection, though, the headmasters agreed that it might be correct. Many reasons were given for the high incomes including the fact that both parents often work and that the soy bean crop did especially well last year. It is a matter of speculation as to what will happen to these schools if unemployment increases or if there is a crop failure.

A most interesting fact appears in the answers to items #17 and #18—the parents are poorly informed regarding the amount of help provided by the school in personal and social problems. This is most surprising in light of the parent teacher association activity and the influence it wields (item #35). Well over one-half of the families believe that the parent teacher organization is an important influence

---

Questionnaire B, Continued

28. We feel that the methods which the teachers use are:
    1. up-to-date and acceptable. (1858—62.4%)
    2. do not concentrate enough on the learning of "basic" facts. (404—13.6)
    3. concentrate too much on the "basic" facts and do not offer sufficient change for creativity on the part of the children. (256—8.6%)
    4. we have no opinion. (390—13.1%)
       No response 68 or 2.2%

29. In regard to objectives, the school:
    1. concentrates too much on college preparation. (87—2.9%)
    2. Should have a more varied program so that children will have a greater choice of objectives. (542—18.2%)
    3. has an acceptable program. (1306—43.9%)
    4. has a good program. (671—22.5%)
    5. we have no opinion. (342—11.5%)
       No response 28 or 0.9%

30. We believe that in regard to textbooks, the school, in general:
    1. makes good choices. (1826—61.4%)
    2. should use fewer textbooks and increase the materials available in the classrooms. (80—2.7%)
    3. should use more supplementary materials from the library and elsewhere. (165—5.5%)
    4. should use a greater variety of textbooks to provide materials for both slow and fast learners. (512—17.2%)
    5. we have no opinion. (360—12.1%)
       No response 33 or 1.1%

---

in the school. This is very much in contrast to the responses of public school parents to the same item.

It also is interesting to note that the feelings of the parents toward their private schools shows through in many ways. For example, when asked their opinions of the length of the school day, the opening hour of the school, the length of the school year, and the amount of time available for the lunch hour, the average private school parent expressed far more satisfaction than than usually expressed by public school parents *in spite* of very similar school calendars and daily schedules.

These parents are also more enthusiastic in their response to the amount of information the schools provide about their children's progress and the value of extracurricular activities than are public school parents. Even in areas of the greatest weakness of the schools, the parents give the school strong endorsement. For example, the parents believe the amount of choice in schools subjects (item #27) is about right, that the methods of the teachers are up-to-date and acceptable (item #28), that in regard to objectives the schools have an

---

Questionnaire B, Continued

31. In our opinion the school library:
     1. is good. (616—20.7%)
     2. is average. (1124—37.8%)
     3. is poor. (541—18.2%)
     4. we have no opinion. (608—20.4%)
         No response 87 or 2.9%

32. We believe that the teachers are:
     1. well-prepared. (1400—47.0%)
     2. in need of more preparation. (624—21.0%)
     3. out-of-date. (35—1.2%)
     4. well-prepared and desirous of continuing to learn. (521—17.5%)
     5. we have no opinion. (368—12.4%)
         No response 28 or 0.9%

33. We believe that the school campus is:
     1. as attractive as it should be. (934—31.4%)
     2. very attractive. (496—16.7%)
     3. in need of attention. (1197—40.2%)
     4. unimportant. (120—4.0%)
     5. we have no opinion. (195—6.6%)
         No response 34 or 1.1%

---

acceptable program (item #29), that the schools make good choices of textbooks (item #30), that the teachers are well-prepared (item #32), and that academic standards are just about right (item #34). On most of these items observation of trained observers show that the parents are unrealistic in their positive opinions. *The public schools could learn an important lesson from the reactions of the parents of these private schools.* Although public school personnel say that the schools belong to the parents, a large group of parents do not believe this is true and find the schools to be unresponsive to their wishes. Parents, in general, do not believe the schools belong to them and that the school boards hear their suggestions.

A most revealing bit of information is shown in item #25. Over three-fifths of the parents live five or more miles from their school. Additionally, about two-fifths have their children transported to school by school bus (item #37). One of the complaints of these parents about the public schools, though, is the fact that their

---

Questionnaire B, Continued

34. In regard to academic standards we believe:
    1. not enough is required to each student. (445—15.0%)
    2. too much is required of the students. (156—5.2%)
    3. about the right amount is required of each student. (2131—71.6%)
    4. we have no opinion. (195—6.6%)
       No response 49 or 1.6%

35. We believe that the parent-teacher association is:
    1. an important influence in the school. (1689—56.8%)
    2. should play a more important part in the school. (425—14.3%)
    3. should be consulted more. (223—7.5%)
    4. is consulted too much. (66—2.2%)
    5. we have no opinion. (527—17.7%)
       No response 46 or 1.5%

36. The amount of money we spent this year for textbooks for each child in this grade group was:
    1. less than $5.00. (460—15.5%)
    2. $5.00 to $9.99. (290—9.7%)
    3. $10.00 to $14.99. (457—15.4%)
    4. $15.00 to $19.99. (416—14.0)
    5. $20.00 or more. (1177—39.5%)
       No response 176 or 5.9%

37. The child we have described gets to school:
    1. by walking or riding a bicycle. (88—3.0)
    2. we drive him to school or he rides in a carpool. (1428—48.0)
    3. by school bus. (1159—38.9)
    4. by public transportation. (33—1.1%)
    5. he drives an automobile. (223—7.5%)
       No response 45 or 1.5%

---

children are transported long distances to achieve a social goal. Apparently, it is less harmful to transport the children for goals sought by the parents than for goals sought by "society."

On some points the parents are realistic. They see the campuses as in need of attention and believe the libraries are average.

When presented with five alternatives (item #39) and asked to select the most important reason for sending children to their school, the parents were very much of "one mind." About 66 per cent said the most important reason was because the children learn more than in the public schools. When asked to select the second most important reason, there was little agreement although the largest number said it was because the discipline is better.

The Parent Inventory indicates that the average parent has more positive attitudes toward these private schools than parents hold toward the public schools. However, some of these schools have

---

Questionnaire B, Continued

38. If you pay to have your child transported to school, please indicate how much you pay per month, per child.
   1. We do not pay to have him transported. (1462—49.1%)
   2. Less than $5.00 (101—3.4%)
   3. $5.00 to $9.99. (323—10.9%)
   4. $10.00 to $14.99. (598—20.1)
   5. $15.00 or more. (366—12.3%)
      No response 126 or 4.2%

39. Of the following we believe the *most* important reason we had for sending our child to this school was:
   1. He will learn more than in the public schools. (1956—65.7%)
   2. He will receive a Christian education. (527—17.7%)
   3. He can be with people like himself. (271—9.1)
   4. Because the discipline is better in this school. (110—3.7%)
   5. Because our family, our friends, or other people in our community were doing it or wanted us to do it. (51—1.7%)
      No response 61 or 2.0%

40. Of the reasons listed in #39, which was the *second most* important?
   1. He will learn more than in the public schools. (634—21.3%)
   2. He will receive a Christian education. (624—21.0%)
   3. He can be with people like himself. (542—18.2%)
   4. Because the discipline is better in this school. (963—32.4%)
   5. Because our family, our friends, or other people in our community were doing it or wanted us to do it. (128—4.3%)
      No response 85 or 2.9%

---

parents with below average attitudes and many of the public schools surpass the schools in this study.

A second finding is that the same decline noted for attitudes toward the public schools as children go from grade to grade is also present in the private schools although not to the same degree as in the public schools.

A third finding is that parents strive for moral absolutes, are concrete in their thinking, and can be classed as middle-class moralists. They see morality as Christian and equate both absolute morality and Christianity with the "American Way of Life."

A fourth finding is that the parents are not prepared to see the weakness in their schools. They either are poor judges of quality in schools or are blind to the faults of their schools. Quite likely this is because they know they own the schools and the schools are more responsive to them as they must be to survive. There is a valuable lesson here for the public schools.

Feelings About Schools

Every child grades 4-12 was administered the Feelings About

QUESTIONNAIRE C

FEELINGS ABOUT SCHOOL

This is not a test since we want only to know what you believe or how you feel about certain things. What you say will be held in strictest confidence and no one in your school will be told what you said. You can help your school to improve itself by being as honest as you can be. Please be as fair as is possible.

(On the form below, the numbers in the first column indicate the number of people who responded by saying **true**, and the percentage they formed. The number and percentage in the second column are those people who responded by saying **false**.)

1.	I am learning things in school which help me now.	3133 (88.5%)	409 (11.5%)
2.	The students are given a square deal in most of the school activities.	2603 (73.5%)	940 (26.5%]
3.	Too many of our teachers have pets.	1719 (48.5%)	1825 (51.5%)
4.	Mostly, I like our school clubs and activities.	2538 (71.7%)	1003 (28.3%)
5.	The teachers pick on some of the kids.	2124 (59.9%)	1421 (40.1%)
6.	I like the way our teachers treat us.	2043 (57.7%)	1499 (42.3%)
7.	Some of the teachers are lazy.	1405 (39.6%)	2141 (60.4%)
8.	I hate one of my teachers.	1666 (47.0%)	1879 (53.0%)
9.	Our teachers are interested in us.	2701 (76.3%)	838 (23.7%)

142

School instrument (Questionnaire C), which is a 50-item attitude scale. This attachment lists the responses of 3,551 students. These students had an average score of 11.7 which is significantly more positive than the average score of 5.1 found in the public schools; thus, the positive attitudes of the parents resemble those of the students.

Differences in scores were examined among the schools. It was determined that the schools vary significantly from each other; some are below the average of the public school group while others are considerably above that average.

Repeatedly it is found in the public schools that girls have more positive attitudes towards their schools than do boys. The same is true for the private schools. The average score of the boys was 9.8 and for the girls was 13.4. It should be noted that the average score of the boys, although less than that of the girls, was still above the average score of all students in the public schools. Boys feel that teachers discriminate against them more than they do against girls. Boys also report that teachers are more demanding of them and, at

Questionnaire C, Continued

10.	When we have assembly programs, they are usually interesting.	2501 (70.6%)	1041 (29.4%)
11.	My classes are boring.	1720 (48.6%)	1821 (51.4%)
12.	Our teachers are not interested in our school organizations.	660 (18.6%)	2881 (81.4%)
13.	Our student leaders are interested in doing a good job.	2768 (78.2%)	770 (21.8%)
14.	Some of my classes are so uninteresting that I cannot do my best work.	2211 (62.5%)	1329 (37.5%)
15.	My teachers usually have a good sense of humor.	2739 (77.4%)	800 (22.6%)
16.	In general, I like my teachers.	3024 (85.5%)	513 (14.5%)
17.	My teachers try to understand me.	2381 (67.3%)	1157 (32.7%)
18.	Some of my teachers are not very happy about being teachers.	1010 (28.6%)	2523 (71.4%)
19.	My teachers are seldom sarcastic.	2045 (57.8%)	1496 (42.2%)
20.	I would not be going to school if I did not have to.	873 (24.6%)	2671 (75.4%)
21.	School work is boring and uninteresting for me.	1342 (38.0%)	2191 (62.0%)
22.	My teachers usually make me feel as if I am important.	1515 (42.8%)	2027 (57.2%)
23.	My teachers like me.	2676 (75.7%)	861 (24.3%)
24.	My teachers are honest with me.	2989 (84.5%)	548 (15.5%)

times, more negative toward them. The situation appears to be the same in both the public and the private schools.

It has also been noted in the public schools that there is a rapid and regular decrease in positive attitude toward the schools as the children go from grade to grade. The same differences among grades is noted in the private school group and significant differences are present among the grades. However, in the public schools, the decline begins in the fourth grade and continues through grades 11 or 12 without significant change. In the private school group the high of 27.0 was in grade 4 and the scores show rapid change to a low of 4.5 in grade 8. From grade 8 through 12 there is a gradual increase to a score of 12.0 in grade 12. The most likely explanation is that in the public schools there is a more gradual introduction to departmentalization and subject matter specialization than in these private schools. Subject matter concentration begins earlier in the private schools and the reaction is far more negative. It should be remembered that from the point of view of the school personnel, the primary purpose of these schools is college preparation.

Questionnaire C, Continued

25.	Some of the women teachers show favoritism towards boys in their classes.	**2331** (65.8%)	**1213** (34.2%)
26.	Some teachers assign unreasonable amounts of homework.	**2119** (59.8%)	**1427** (40.2%)
27.	Most of the teachers are fair in their criticisms of my work.	**2955** (83.4%)	**588** (16.6%)
28.	Some of the teachers act as if they were bored with their work.	**1373** (38.7%)	**2173** (61.3%)
29.	Some of the teachers act as if they want the students to feel embarrassed.	**1793** (50.7%)	**1746** (49.3%)
30.	I like most of the courses I have taken at this school.	**2536** (71.5%)	**1009** (28.5%)
31.	Some of the teachers act as if they want the students to be afraid of them.	**1740** (49.1%)	**1804** (50.9%)
32.	Most of the teachers are pleasant and cheerful most of the time.	**2640** (74.5%)	**902** (25.5%)
33.	Most of the teachers try to be fair in dealing with students.	**2931** (82.8%)	**608** (17.2%)
34.	Some of my teachers do not grade fairly.	**1262** (35.6%)	**2278** (64.4%)
35.	Some of my courses are extremely boring.	**2334** (66.0%)	**1203** (34.0%)
36.	We are not given enough freedom in choosing our courses.	**1898** (53.8%)	**1630** (46.2%)
37.	My textbooks are up-to-date.	**2468** (69.8%)	**1068** (30.2%)
38.	Our teachers do not pay enough attention to what we are interested in.	**1969** (55.7%)	**1568** (44.3%)

Locus of Responsibility Scale. The Locus of Responsibility Scale was administered to all students in grades 4-12. This instrument contains 27 items and seeks to answer the question, "Who is making the decisions in this classroom?" The instrument can be scored and the responses of students to each of the items can be tabulated. A copy of the instrument with the items tabulated for the entire group of 3,569 students is attached.

The Locus of Responsibility Scale yields three scores. These scores are measures of teacher-centeredness, interaction, and student-centeredness. In other words, the scores are measures of the extent to which teachers make decisions for the students, the degree to which teachers interact with students in making decisions, and the degree to which they permit students to make decisions for themselves.

In the public schools the average teacher-centered score is 19.2, the average for interaction is 16.3, and the average for student-centeredness is 8.1. For the private schools the averages in the same order were: 20.1, 17.7, and 6.6. Thus, in the private schools, in con-

---

Questionnaire C, Continued

39.	The food prices are usually fair.	1730 (49.1%)	1795 (50.9%)
40.	Our principal is usually glad to receive suggestions from the students.	2435 (69.0%)	1096 (31.0%)
41.	This school places too much emphasis on grades.	1727 (48.9%)	1804 (51.1%)
42.	There are no student activities at this school which I find interesting.	669 (18.9%)	2868 (81.1%)
43.	There is not enough chance to meet other students and become friends with them during the school day.	1580 (44.6%)	1960 (55.4%)
44.	Our student council tries to help the students.	2052 (59.0%)	1425 (41.0%)
45.	I like the way this school is run.	1691 (47.9%)	1842 (52.1%)
46.	Some of the men teachers show favoritism toward girls in their classes.	2098 (59.3%)	1439 (40.7%)
47.	It is hard to get along at this school unless you are someone's pet.	1102 (31.2%)	2435 (68.8%)
48.	It is difficult for a new student to get to know other people at this school.	1207 (34.2%)	2327 (65.8%)
49.	It would be easy to organize a new club at this school.	1944 (55.0%)	1590 (45.0%)
50.	Students get square deals even if they are being punished for breaking school rules.	1740 (49.3%)	1790 (50.7%)

---

trast to the public schools, the teachers make more decisions for the students and with the students but permit the students to make fewer decisions by themselves. Basically, the private schools establish a relationship with students which is more autocratic and it appears that the higher level of interaction is the result of greater student tractability and the smaller size of the average class. Teachers and students have a closer relationship in the private schools because of class size, size of the school, and the fact that a teacher may teach a child in several classes.

It is important to note that even though students in the private schools tend to be more highly dominated by their teachers than those in the public schools, the attitudes toward school of the private school students remain more positive. Quite likely this is because the relationships these students have with adults, for instance their parents and church leaders, is an authoritarian relationship (and not in the worst sense of the term) which they have come to accept as part of a middle-class way of life and a "Christian" way of life.

In the public schools it is noted that teachers are more direct

---

QUESTIONNAIRE D

LOCUS OF RESPONSIBILITY SCALE

Dear student. Please respond to the following statements so that we can have a better understanding of how you see the class you have been asked to describe. There are no "right" or "wrong" answers so please respond only as you see things. To answer the items, read each item and then select the response which seems to you to best describe the class. Please select only one answer for an item. On the answer sheet opposite the number of the item, blacken in the number of the answer you have selected. Please make your mark with a number 2 black lead pencil. Make your mark heavy and only as long as the lines. If you make an error or wish to change your answer, erase completely. Please make no 'stray' marks on the answer sheet.

1. Planning for what will be done in this class is done
   1. Almost entirely by the teacher.   1506 (42.2%)
   2. Mostly by the teacher.   942 (26.4%)
   3. Partly by the teacher and partly by the students.   986 (27.6%)
   4. Mostly by the students.   75 (2.1%)
   5. Almost entirely by the students.   60 (1.7%)

2. What we will study in this class is determined
   1. Almost entirely by the teacher.   1857 (52.1%)
   2. Largely by the teacher.   1146 (32.1%)
   3. Partly by us and partly by the teacher.   491 (13.8%)
   4. Largely by us.   43 (1.2%)
   5. Almost entirely by us.   30 (.8%)

---

with male students, interact more with female students, and leave male students more frequently to their own devices as shown by student-centeredness scores. Significant differences were present in all three of the Locus of Responsibility Scale scores for the private schools when the averages for males and females were compared. Teachers were more direct with males (means of 20.4 and 19.6), interacted more with females (means of 16.9 and 18.4), and left male students to their own devices (ignored or overlooked) more frequently (means of 7.0 and 6.5). Thus, the typical middle-class pattern of a female dominated society is found to exist in the schools. This finding should be coupled with the fact that the large majority of teachers in the private schools which were studied were female.

It has been noted that in the public schools teacher-centeredness increases regularly from grades 4 through 12. At the same time, interaction between student and teacher decreases. No regular changes in student-centeredness occurs. All three of the Locus of Responsibility Scale scores showed significant differences among the grades for the private schools although there was no regular pattern

---

Questionnaire D, Continued

3. How this class is run is decided
   1. Almost entirely by us.   142 (4.0%)
   2. Largely by us.   86 (2.4%)
   3. Partly by us and partly by the teacher.   682 (19.1%)
   4. Largely by the teacher.   1156 (32.4%)
   . Almost entirely by the teacher.   1499 (42.0%)

4. In terms of what he (she) does in this class, the teacher seems to believe that responsibility for what happens is
   1. Almost entirely his (hers).   706 (20.0%)
   2. Largely his.   642 (18.2%)
   3. Partly his and partly ours.   1403 (39.8%)
   4. Largely ours.   441 (12.5%)
   5. Almost entirely ours.   331 (9.4%)

5. Most of the time in this class the talking is done:
   1. Almost entirely by the teacher.   542 (15.2%)
   2. Mostly by the teacher.   591 (16.6%)
   3. Partly by the teacher and partly by us.   1726 (48.4%)
   5. Mostly by us.   459 (12.9%]
   5. Almost entirely by us.   248 (7.0%)

---

discerned for differences in student-centered scores. Teacher centeredness was relatively low in grade four and decreased through grade six. In grade seven it increased significantly and continued to increase in grade eight. From grade eight through grade twelve there was a significant regular decline but the grade twelve average was still above that of grades 4-7.

Interaction trends were the reverse of the teacher-centered trends. Interaction increases through grade six, decreases in grades seven and eight, and then continues to increase through grade 12. Grade 12, however, shows a lower average than grade five.

Two generalizations can be made. First, the greatest opportunity the students in the private schools will have to participate in making decisions for themselves is in grades 4 through 6. As they mature they will have less opportunity to do this. Second, something enters the relationship of teacher to student in the middle grades which leads the teachers to become more direct and authoritarian with the students and to interact less with them in making decisions. At the same time, and as shown by the Feelings About

---

Questionnaire D, Continued

6. Decisions about how much we have done and how well we have done which are used to decide our grades in this class are made:

1. Almost entirely by us.	147	(4.1%)
2. Mostly by us.	105	(2.9%)
3. Partly by us and partly by the teacher.	389	(10.9%)
4. Mostly by the teacher.	982	(27.5%)
5. Almost entirely by the teacher.	1944	(54.5%)

7. How we will study something in this class is decided:

1. Almost entirely by us.	181	(5.1%)
2. Largely by us.	190	(5.4%)
3. Partly by us and partly by the teacher.	848	(24.0%)
4. Largely by the teacher.	1092	(31.0%)
5. Almost entirely by the teacher.	1215	(34.5%)

8. In this class the teacher gives his ideas:

1. Most of the time.	684	(19.2%)
2. Very often but sometimes we can give ours.	1462	(41.1%)
3. Whenever he thinks he has something to contribute to the discussion.	991	(27.8%)
4. When we ask him for them.	247	(6.9%)
5. Almost never.	176	(4.9%)

School, there is a significant shift in the attitudes the students hold toward the schools. As the teachers become more direct, the students' feelings become more negative.

Scores of the 11 schools were compared and again proved to show significant differences among the schools. Some of the schools were less direct and more interactive than others. Some were less direct and more interactive than many of the public schools although the average showed greater teacher domination.

Relationship Inventory. The 72 item Relationship Inventory was administered to all students in grades 6-12. A copy of the instrument with tabulations of the 2,934 students who responded appears as Questionnaire E on pp. 156-161.

The Relationship Inventory is an instrument which enables students to describe the quality of relationships they have with a interpersonal relationship qualities which are believed to be both necessary and sufficient for helping to promote the personal growth of people. Much research exists to show that when teachers are empathic in their understanding of students, when they regard their

---

Questionnaire D, Continued

9. The teacher asks questions
   1. To see if we know the answers.   **1016**   (28.5%)
   2. To see if we have studied.   **1705**   (47.8%]
   3. To start a discussion.   **493**   (13.8%)
   4. Seldom.   **235**   (6.6%)
   5. Almost never.   **119**   (3.3%)

10. When we speak in class
    1. The teacher always lets us know if he thinks we are right of wrong.   **1180**   (33.1%)
    2. The teacher usually lets us know if he thinks we are right or wrong.   **1211**   (34.2%)
    3. The teacher may respond or he may let one of us talk.   **877**   (24.6%)
    4. If there is a response, it is most often made by one of us.   **201**   (5.6%)
    5. No response is made unless some student makes it.   **159**   (4.5%)

11. The teacher acts as if
    1. We can make up our minds for ourselves.   **616**   (17.3%)
    2. We can usually make up our minds for ourselves.   **742**   (20.9%)
    3. He should help when we need it or are having a problem in deciding and leave us alone otherwise.   **1499**   (42.1%)
    4. He should take the lead in deciding what we should think.   **394**   (11.1%)
    5. He should be responsible for what we think in this class.   **306**   (8.6%)

---

students as important people, when they do not place conditions on their regard for their students, and when they are congruent in their relationships with their students, these students move toward greater openness to their experience and a more effective use of the potentials they possess.

The term empathy is used here to describe a relationship in which the student believes his teacher understands what it is like to be the student—that the teacher can "walk around in the shoes of the student." Positiveness of regard merely means that from the point of view of the student, his teacher acts as if he believes that the student is an important person. If a teacher is unconditional in his regard for a student, it seems to the student that the teacher is not placing a "price" on his positive regard, saying in effect, "I will regard you highly if you are the kind of person I value and will not regard you highly if you are different." And by congruence it is meant that the student perceives his teacher to be thinking and feeling in a manner consistent with how he (the teacher) is behaving—the teacher does

---

Questionnaire D, Continued

12. In regard to our personal thoughts and feelings about what is being discussed, the teacher believes
   1. He should decide them for us.   **352** (9.9%)
   2. He should influence them to some degree to make them like his.   **595** (16.8%)
   3. We should discuss things together and make up our minds for ourselves.   **1858** (52.4%)
   4. He should influence our thoughts and feelings only to a small degree.   **445** (12.5%)
   5. He should never influence our thoughts and feelings.   **298** (8.4%)

13. As far as what we study, the teacher seems
   1. To want to decide for us what we will think.   **509** (14.4%)
   2. Usually to want to decide for us what we will think.   **389** (11.0%)
   3. To want to help us decide for ourselves what we will think.   **1211** (34.2%)
   4. To want us to decide for ourselves with some help from him.   **1087** (30.7%)
   5. To want us to decide for ourselves without any help from him.   **346** (9.8%)

not give the appearance of thinking and feeling one way and talking or behaving as if he were thinking and feeling in another way.

The norms for the Relationship Inventory show that teachers find it easier to have a high level of regard and to be congruent with students than to understand them empathically or to set no conditions on their expression of regard. The norm averages are: Level of Regard 9.3, Empathic Understanding 3.0, Unconditionality of Regard 1.2, and Congruence 8.8. The same pattern of scores was shown for the private schools but scores were significantly different in magnitude. For the private schools the average scores in the same order as above were 12.3, 4.3, 1.3, and 12.5. Thus, there was a higher level of regard of teachers for students in the private schools and a greater congruence on the part of the teachers. At the same time there was a slightly larger amount of empathic understanding in the private schools. Both groups were highly conditional in their expression of regard, rewarding students only when they behaved in a manner approved by the teacher.

Questionnaire D, Continued

14. To make the class interesting
    1. The teacher almost always relies on himself.   534 (15.0%)
    2. The teacher usually relies on himself.   599 (16.8%)
    3. The teacher works closely with us and our ideas.   1809 (50.8%)
    4. The teacher usually relies on us.   390 (11.0%)
    5. The teacher almost always relies on us.   227 (6.4%)

15. The teacher has plans for the class which he brings to class and
    1. Always follows.   672 (18.9%)
    2. Almost always follows.   1134 (31.9%)
    3. Usually follows but changes his plans when we have something important to suggest.   1302 (36.6%)
    4. Frequently does not follow because we want to do something else.   189 (5.3%)
    5. Hardly ever follows because we usually get him off the subject.   263 (7.4%)

16. The teacher seems to feel that the personal meanings of discussions to students are
    1. Unimportant.   425 (11.9%)
    2. Of little value.   576 (16.2%)
    3. Of some value and encourages us to discuss our personal meanings.   1994 (56.0%)
    4. More important than what he has to say.   366 (10.3%)
    5. Much more important than what he has to say.   198 (5.6%)

The four scores were examined for differences among the 11 schools. As with the other instruments, significant differences were present for each of the four scores, adding to the conclusion that these schools do not constitute a homeogeneous group; they differ significantly from each other.

With the exception of the congruence scores, no differences are usually found when the scores of males are compared with those of females. Males report that their teachers are less open and congruent in their relationships with them than is reported by females. The same pattern was present for the private schools except that for the congruence scores there were greater differences than in the public schools. In other words, in the private schools there is an even greater difference in the congruence of teachers perceived by males and females than in the public schools. Does the greater aggressiveness of the male students bother the teachers? Is there some other reason?

In the public schools no significant differences are found in any of the scores when they are examined by grade levels. The same is

---

Questionnaire D, Continued

17. The teacher directs a student's work
    1. Never.   232   (6.5%)
    2. Only after the student requests direction.   1070   (30.0%)
    3. When he senses that the student needs it.   1345   (37.7%)
    4. After the student has tried for himself but before the
       student requests direction.   717   (20.1%)
    5. Before the student has a chance to try for himself.   203   (5.7%)

18. The amount of work the students do seems to be
    1. Chiefly what the teacher wishes.   1670   (46.9%)
    2. Mostly what the teacher wishes and a little of what the
       students wish.   947   (26.6%)
    3. Partly what the teacher wishes and partly what the
       students wish.   635   (17.8%)
    4. A little that the teacher wishes and mostly what the
       students wish.   177   (5.0%)
    5. Chiefly what the students wish.   131   (3.7%)

19. The classroom procedure is
    1. Chiefly lecture.   708   (19.9%)
    2. Mostly lecture with little discussion.   955   (26.8%)
    3. Some lecture and some discussion.   1211   (34.0%)
    4. A little lecture and mostly discussion.   322   (9.0%)
    5. Chiefly discussion.   365   (10.2%]

---

not true for the private schools and regular significant differences are present among the grades on each of the scores. In each case the trend is identical to that of the other scores and closely resembles the trends shown by the Feelings About School and the Locus of Responsibility Scale. Thus, scores decrease from grade 6 through grade 8 and then increase to grade 12. The lowest point invariably is grade 8. The grade 8 averages were: Level of Regard 4.8, Empathic Understanding -.7, Unconditionality of Regard -1.0 and congruence 9.0. With the exception of the congruence average, these are very low scores as can be seen by comparing them with the norm averages above.

A consistent pattern is thus to be seen for the three instruments. This pattern is for high and positive scores to be present (with the exception of the teacher-centeredness score on the Locus of Responsibility Scale) but for the averages to decline through grade 8 and then to improve through grade 12. Something must occur in perceptions of children or in anxieties in the relationships which cause teachers to be less accepting of these middle grade students, to be

---

Questionnaire D, Continued

20. We can talk with each other in class
    1. Almost always.   373   (10.5%)
    2. Most of the time.   433   (12.2%)
    3. Whenever it does not disrupt what is going on. 1494   (42.1%)
    4. Very little of the time.   649   (18.3%)
    5. Almost never.   600   (16.9%)

21. We are given a chance to express our ideas
    1. Practically never.   255   (7.2%)
    2. Seldom.   410   (11.6%)
    3. Whenever it fits what we are doing.   1685   (47.5%)
    4. Very often.   665   (18.8%)
    5. Almost always.   530   (15.0%)

22. The teacher insists that we stick to the subject matter of the class
    1. Practically always.   1334   (37.7%)
    2. Usually.   1301   (36.7%)
    3. Sometimes.   614   (17.3%)
    4. Very seldom.   175   (4.9%)
    5. Practically never.   118   (3.3%)

153

more dictatorial with them, and to set greater demands on them for expression of regard. It may well be that the greater dependence of the elementary school children and the greater maturity of the high school students make it easier for teachers to trust them and to relate satisfactorily to them but the striving for greater autonomy and self determination of the pre-adolescent seriously disturbs that relationship.

Questionnaire D, Continued

23. What a student does tends to reflect his particular interests
    1. Hardly at all.   372   (10.5%)
    2. A little.   677   (19.1%)
    3. As far as his interests can be reflected in this course.   1448   (40.8%)
    4. A great deal.   760   (21.4%)
    5. Almost all of the time.   293   (8.3%)

24. The conclusions which are arrived at in this class are
    1. Usually those of the teacher.   842   (23.7%)
    2. Frequently those of the teacher.   491   (13.8%)
    3. Sometimes the teacher's and sometimes our own.   1900   (53.5%)
    4. Frequently our own.   170   (4.8%)
    5. Usually our own.   149   (4.2%)

25. How much we will know and how hard we have to work at it is decided
    1. Almost entirely by the teacher.   918   (25.8%)
    2. Mostly by the teacher.   999   (28.1%)
    3. By both the students and the teacher.   1131   (31.8%)
    4. Mostly by the students.   308   (8.7%)
    5. Almost entirely by the students.   202   (5.7%)

26. How far we will go in this class is determined
    1. Chiefly by the students.   290   (8.1%)
    2. A little by the teacher but mostly by the students.   298   (8.4%]
    3. Partly by the students and partly by the teacher.   779   (21.9%)
    4. A little by the students but mostly by the teacher.   851   (23.9%)
    5. Chiefly by the teacher.   1341   (37.7%)

27. The teacher
    1. Tells us what we should know.   1315   (37.4%)
    2. Tells us what he (she) believes we should know but lets us do some thinking for ourselves.   1004   (28.6%)
    3. Tries to help us discover what we think and what other people have thought about the same thing.   764   (21.7%)
    4. Sometimes tells us what he (she) believes but is more interested in what we believe.   278   (7.9%)
    5. Is mostly interested in what we believe.   154   (4.4%)

4

Students' Attitudes Toward Themselves

Three levels of the Index of Adjustment and Values (IAV) were used in the study: the Elementary IAV (grades 3-5), Junior High IAV (grades 6-8), and High School IAV (grades 9-12). Each of these levels of the IAV yields a number of important scores including self concept and ideal self (a measure of level of aspiration and also a measure of motivation to do school work), concept of other people, acceptance of others, concept of other people's ideals, discrepancy between other people's self concepts and their ideal selves, and a measure of adjustment. In the discussion which follows only those scores which appear to have significance are stressed. (The actual instruments and scores are not included in this book since they do not lend themselves to interpretation in their raw form.)

One of the more important scores of the IAV is derived from the relationship between acceptance of self and acceptance of others. These two scores can be used to develop four categories of people: + +, − +, + −, and − −. In each of the four groups, the first sign relates to self and the second to others. Thus, a + + person is one who is accepting of his own worth and is at least equally valuing of the worth of other people. The − + person questions his own worth and values other people above himself. He does not believe he is a worthy person. The + − values himself above other people; believes he has more worth than other people (or at least he gives the appearance of holding these views—actually, the +— person suffers from strong feelings of inferiority which are hidden from himself and from other people by his strong attention away from himself). And the —— person rejects the worth of both himself and of other people. Thus, the ++ person values himself and other people; the —+ believes that other people are more acceptable; the +— acts as if he were more acceptable than other people; and the —— person rejects both his own worth and that of other people.

Obviously, there are distinct personality and learning problems in each of the groups. The —+ person is retiring and non self-assertive. He suffers misgivings about his efforts and believes that he is not a capable person. He hesitates to try for fear of failure and to protect himself against failure, he may concentrate on the details of problems rather than the problems themselves.

The +— person, though, blames his problems on other people. He has no reluctance to try anything and if he fails he either does not recognize it or he is able to dismiss himself from the blame. He is self

---

QUESTIONNAIRE E

RELATIONSHIP INVENTORY

(Please note that discussion of this instrument appears on pp. 149-154.)

Below are listed some ways that a person may feel or behave toward another person. Please consider each statement carefully with reference to your relationship with (the teacher).

Mark each statement according to how strongly you feel it is true, or not true, in this relationship. Please mark every one. Write in plus (+) or (—) marks to stand for the following answers:

+ + +   Yes, I strongly feel that it is true.

+ +   Yes, I feel it is true.

+   Yes, I feel that it is probably true or more than untrue.

—   No, I feel that it is probably untrue or more untrue than untrue.

——   No, I feel it is not true.

———   No, I strongly feel that is not true.

---

assertive and tends to be domineering. He is basically uncertain of himself and insecure but he defends himself against these feelings so well that he seldom is aware of them. He defends himself by living his life outside himself. He is a stranger to himself.

Another score which should be amplified to communicate its meaning is the score which is derived from nothing the differences between the self concept rating and the ideal self concept rating for each trait of the IAV and summing these for all of the traits on the IAV. Such a scoring technique causes people to be placed in one of two groups: those who endorse the traits of the IAV and those who reject the traits of the IAV. The first of these two groups is called the positive self-ideal discrepancy and the second the negative self-ideal discrepancy. It is important to realize that the traits on the three levels of the IAV used in the study are those which are endorsed overwhelmingly by teachers. Negative self-ideal discrepant students are in conflict with their teachers.

Students with negative self-ideal discrepancies have been found to be less highly motivated to do good school work and to have more

---

Questionnaire E, Continued

In this table the first row of numbers shows the actual number of students who chose each response, and the second is the percentage choosing each response.

		+++	++	+	−	− −	− − −
1.	He (she) respects me.	588	944	838	225	178	162
		20.0	32.2	28.6	7.7	6.1	5.5
2.	He (she) tries to understand exactly how I see things.	549	816	747	319	267	235
		18.7	27.8	25.5	10.9	9.1	8.0
3.	He (she) is interested in me only when I am talking about certain things.	372	487	475	431	690	465
		12.7	16.7	16.3	14.8	23.6	15.9
4.	He (she) tells me things that he does not mean.	187	209	220	353	794	1135
		6.5	7.2	7.6	12.2	27.4	39.2
5.	He (she) disapproves of me.	201	154	224	438	837	1009
		7.0	5.4	7.8	15.3	29.2	35.2
6.	He (she) understands my words but does not know how I feel.	438	521	584	451	577	350
		15.0	17.8	20.0	15.4	19.8	12.0
7.	Sometimes he (she) is more friendly toward me than he (she) is at other times.	863	935	440	205	286	195
		29.5	32.0	15.0	7.0	9.8	6.7
8.	What he (she) says to me is never different from what he (she) thinks or feels.	619	682	672	382	320	237
		21.3	23.4	23.1	13.1	11.0	8.1
9.	He (she) is curious about what makes me act like I do, but not really interested in me as a person.	317	331	377	524	679	680
		10.9	11.4	13.0	18.0	23.3	23.4
10.	He (she) is interested in knowing how things seem to me.	440	709	573	394	397	380
		15.2	24.5	19.8	13.6	13.7	13.1
11.	His (her) feeling toward me is not due to the way that I am reacting to him (her).	438	630	655	411	428	312
		15.2	21.9	22.8	14.3	14.9	10.9

---

negative feelings about school than other students. One reason for this may be because these students do not aspire to be the kind of people valued by their teachers. Teachers idealize the type of traits included on the IAV and the presence or absence of these traits in their students tends to make a significant differences in how they be-have toward students. Students who value being cheerful, neat, obedient, polite, quiet, studious, tactful, truthful, etc. (these are traits such as those used on the IAV) are more highly accepted by their teachers than students who do not value these traits to the same degree. It is for this reason that girls usually achieve greater success and acceptance in schools than do boys. The child who aspires to have these traits is usually the child who is aspiring to be the kind of person the teacher will accept and reward. To be successful in our schools, students must aspire to be the kind of people their teachers desire unless they have talents well above the average that help them achieve success without the acceptance of their teachers. (This state-ment is not meant to be an endorsement of that state of affairs, only to recognize its existence.) The child who desires to be something dif-

Questionnaire E, Continued

		+ + +	+ +	+	−	− −	− − −
12.	He (she) is upset whenever I talk about or ask about certain things.	349 12.0	265 9.1	313 10.8	366 12.6	761 26.2	856 29.4
13.	He (she) likes to see me.	286 9.8	508 17.4	1104 37.7	430 14.7	224 7.7	374 12.8
14.	He (she) nearly always knows exactly what I mean.	394 13.5	715 24.5	755 25.9	408 14.0	352 12.1	293 10.0
15.	He (she) likes me when I feel certain ways about myself but when I feel other ways he (she) does not like me.	200 6.9	245 8.5	533 18.4	672 23.2	652 22.5	596 20.6
16.	He (she) has feelings about me that he (she) does not say anything about and these make it harder for us to get along.	312 10.8	277 9.6	392 13.6	554 19.2	689 23.9	662 22.9
17.	He (she) hardly notices me.	312 10.7	222 7.6	371 12.8	493 17.0	749 25.8	759 26.1
18.	At times he (she) thinks that I feel more strongly or more concerned about something than I do.	306 10.5	566 19.4	729 25.0	620 21.3	452 15.5	242 8.3
19.	He (she) always seems to feel the same way toward me.	611 20.8	796 27.2	701 23.9	333 11.4	278 9.5	212 7.2
20.	He (she) behaves just the way that he (she) really is when I am around.	715 24.5	835 28.6	672 23.0	267 9.1	211 7.2	222 7.6
21.	He (she) appreciates me.	336 11.5	584 20.0	961 32.9	426 14.6	266 9.1	349 11.9
22.	Sometimes he (she) thinks that I feel a certain way, because that is the way he feels.	261 9.0	450 15.5	654 22.5	656 22.6	534 18.4	350 12.0
23.	He (she) likes me in some ways and dislikes me in others.	510 17.6	584 20.1	785 27.0	456 15.7	311 10.7	259 8.9

ferent from what his teacher will reward and accept starts out in school with an automatic problem. Frequently, students who do not possess the characteristics admired by their teachers are rejected, directed by their teachers in an effort to mold them to be more like the teachers' ideals, unrecognized for their talents, and subject to rules and regulations that make little sense to them. A most outstanding problem for the negative self-ideal student is the fact that teachers assign him marks which are lower than his ability *and* his achievement warrant. Obviously, school is not a happy place for the negative self-ideal student nor is it designed to help him want to achieve his best.

Elementary IAV. The Elementary IAV was given to all children in grades 3-5 of the 11 schools. When the scores of the private school children were compared with the norm averages, no great discrepancies were found but several of the differences are worthy of note.

The first difference noted was that on acceptance of self, the private school children were lower than the norm group. This is to say that the private school children do not believe they have as much

---

Questionnaire E, Continued

		+ + +	+ +	+	−	− −	− − −
24.	At times I think he (she) is not aware of the way he (she) feels about me.	265 9.2	398 13.7	632 21.8	704 24.3	527 18.2	369 12.7
25.	He (she) is friendly and warm towards me.	566 19.4	692 23.7	727 24.9	294 10.1	220 7.5	424 14.5
26.	He (she) understands me.	539 18.5	670 23.0	714 24.5	352 12.1	260 8.9	382 13.1
27.	If I am annoyed with him (her), he (she) becomes annoyed with me.	508 17.4	483 16.6	575 19.7	554 19.0	469 16.1	324 11.1
28.	He (she) pretends that he (she) likes me or understands me more than he (she) really does.	258 8.9	323 11.1	456 15.7	648 22.3	682 23.5	536 18.5
29.	He (she) cares about me.	438 15.1	587 20.3	941 32.5	331 11.4	219 7.6	381 13.2
30.	The way he (she) feels about some of the things I say, or do, keeps him (her) from really understanding me.	346 11.9	397 13.6	645 22.1	677 23.2	540 18.5	308 10.6
31.	Whether I am expressing good or bad feelings seems to make no difference to the way he feels about me.	510 17.5	670 23.0	710 24.3	423 14.5	342 11.7	263 9.0
32.	He (she) does not avoid anything that he thinks or feels about me.	318 11.0	593 20.4	920 31.7	567 19.5	333 11.5	170 5.9
33.	He (she) feels that I am dull and uninteresting.	218 7.5	222 7.7	425 14.7	706 24.3	764 26.3	566 19.5
34.	He (she) ignores some of my feelings.	383 13.2	459 15.9	626 21.6	558 19.3	546 18.9	323 11.2
35.	Sometimes he (she) is warm and friendly toward me, at other times cold or disapproving.	419 14.4	466 16.0	569 19.6	481 16.5	517 17.8	455 15.7

---

worth as other children believe they have. A second difference was in concepts of other people. The private school students rated other people higher than they were rated by children in the norm group. This over-rating of other people led to a third difference; the private school children saw other people as closer to their ideals than they are seen by the norm children.

The above differences combine to create a fourth set of differences which relate to the category distributions described above. At this level, children are usually quite accepting of themselves and of other people. In fact, in the norm group about 35 per cent of the children are + +. In contrast, only 28 per cent of the private school children were + +. On the other hand, the norm group contains 27 per cent — + children and the private school group held 39 per cent; a highly significant difference. The private school group also contained fewer + — children and about the same percentage of — — children as the norm group. These comparisons yield the conclusion

---

Questionnaire E, Continued

		+ + +	+ +	+	−	− −	− − −
36.	I feel that I can trust him (her) to be honest with me.	1095	756	483	200	146	238
		37.5	25.9	16.6	6.9	5.0	8.2
37.	He (she) is interested in me.	465	706	891	336	232	289
		15.9	24.2	30.5	11.5	7.9	9.9
38.	He (she) appreciates how my experiences feel to me.	273	607	928	537	297	260
		9.4	20.9	32.0	18.5	10.2	9.0
39.	Depending on the way he (she) feels he (she) sometimes responds to me with quite a lot more warmth and interest than he (she) does at other times.	368	590	870	454	351	271
		12.7	20.3	30.0	15.6	12.1	9.3
40.	He (she) is at ease in our relationship.	421	764	899	343	225	261
		14.5	26.2	30.9	11.8	7.7	9.0
41.	He (she) just puts up with me.	332	306	445	533	667	634
		11.4	10.5	15.3	18.3	22.9	21.7
42.	He (she) tells me what my actions and feelings mean.	188	329	471	611	698	619
		6.4	11.3	16.2	21.0	23.9	21.2
43.	His (her) liking or disliking of me is not affected by anything that I tell him (her) about myself.	465	708	763	433	314	226
		16.0	24.3	26.2	14.9	10.8	7.8
44.	He (she) is acting a part with me.	180	289	489	624	692	620
		6.2	10.0	16.9	21.6	23.9	21.4
45.	He (she) does not really care what becomes of me.	286	250	346	541	653	820
		9.9	8.6	11.9	18.7	22.5	28.3
46.	He (she) does not realize how strongly I feel about some of the things we discuss.	398	520	638	567	465	291
		13.8	18.1	22.2	19.7	16.2	10.1
47.	His (her) general feeling toward me varies a lot.	341	485	666	551	604	257
		11.7	16.7	22.9	19.0	20.8	8.8

---

that the private school children in grades 3-5 do not view themselves as having as much worth as children usually see themselves as having and they believe that other people have more worth than they are usually seen to have.

A fifth difference relates to the percentage of negative self-ideal discrepant children in the two groups. The norm group contains about 7 per cent negative self-ideal discrepant children while the private school children included only about 4 per cent.

Thus, the private school children underrate themselves, overrate other people, and desire to be like the ideals reflected in the Elementary IAV.

Within the private school group, girls' scores were compared to the boys'. Girls had a slightly higher self ideal than the boys but the difference was not statistically significant. However, two other significant differences did appear. Girls in the private school overrate other people to a greater degree than do the boys and the boys have

---

Questionnaire E, Continued

		+++	++	+	−	−−	−−−
48.	Sometimes I feel that what he (she) says to me is quite different from the way he (she) feels underneath.	293 10.1	413 14.2	585 20.2	572 19.7	600 20.7	439 15.1
49.	I feel that he (she) really thinks I am worthwhile.	409 14.0	738 25.3	844 29.0	351 12.1	260 8.9	310 10.6
50.	He (she) responds to me mechanically.	251 8.6	339 11.7	549 18.9	645 22.2	630 21.7	488 16.8
51.	Whether I like or dislike myself makes no difference to the way he (she) feels about me.	446 15.5	715 24.8	775 26.9	431 14.9	330 11.4	187 6.5
52.	I do not think that he (she) is being honest with himself (herself) about the way he (she) feels toward me.	199 6.9	263 9.1	475 16.5	670 23.2	775 26.9	502 17.4
53.	He (she) dislikes me.	295 10.1	169 5.8	282 9.7	507 17.4	755 26.0	899 30.9
54.	He (she) looks at the things I do from his (her) own point of view.	621 21.3	708 24.3	696 23.9	359 12.3	329 11.3	203 7.0
55.	Sometimes he (she) seems to like me and at other times he (she) does not seem to care.	433 14.8	391 13.4	584 20.0	508 17.4	554 19.0	452 15.5
56.	I feel that he (she) is being genuine with me.	503 17.3	743 25.5	820 28.2	383 13.2	246 8.5	215 7.4
57.	He (she) is impatient with me.	315 10.8	274 9.4	385 13.2	550 18.9	826 28.3	566 19.4
58.	He (she) generally sees how I am feeling.	329 11.4	775 26.8	788 27.2	410 14.2	334 11.5	261 9.0
59.	He (she) likes me better when I behave in some ways than he (she) does when I behave in other ways.	582 20.0	815 28.0	764 26.2	343 11.8	233 8.0	176 6.0

---

considerably more negative self-ideal discrepant people in their group than do the girls (5.5 per cent vs. 2.0 per cent).

Junior High School IAV. The Junior High School IAV was given to all children in grades 6-8. When the private school averages were compared with the norm group averages a considerably greater number of differences emerged than when the same comparisons were made for Elementary IAV scores.

In comparison to the norm group, the private school children had lower self concepts, higher self ideals, a greater discrepancy between self and ideal self, higher perceptions of other people's self concepts, higher perceptions of other people's self acceptance, higher ideal others scores, and a smaller difference between others' self concept and others' ideal self. These differences may be summarized to say that the private school children saw themselves as less valuable than other people, had high ideals, and had unrealistically high perceptions of other people.

The above differences acted together to produce significant dif-

---

Questionnaire E, Continued

		+ + +	+ +	+	–	– –	– – –
60.	Sometimes I can see that he (she) is not comfortable with me, but we go on paying no attention to it.	289 10.0	428 14.7	612 21.1	610 21.0	588 20.2	· 377 13.0
61.	He (she) feels a deep liking for me.	238 8.2	439 15.1	869 30.0	531 18.3	342 11.8	481 16.6
62.	He (she) understands completely what I say to him (her).	246 8.5	559 19.3	840 29.0	572 19.7	396 13.7	286 9.9
63.	Whether I feel fine or feel awful makes no difference to how he (she) feels about me.	451 15.6	677 23.4	819 28.3	444 15.3	316 10.9	192 6.6
64.	He (she) does not try to mislead me about his (her) own thoughts or feelings.	477 16.5	818 28.3	839 29.0	323 11.2	257 8.9	176 6.1
65.	He (she) thinks I am disagreeable.	234 8.0	248 8.5	401 13.8	704 24.2	854 29.4	466 16.0
66.	He (she) can be fully aware of the feelings that hurt me most without being upset himself (herself).	391 13.5	596 20.6	855 29.6	502 17.4	333 11.5	216 7.5
67.	I can be very critical of him (her) or I can like him (her) without its changing his (her) feeling toward me.	410 14.1	611 21.0	854 29.4	470 16.2	316 10.9	246 8.5
68.	What he (she) says gives a false impression of his (her) total reaction to me.	196 6.8	258 8.9	529 18.2	756 26.1	769 26.5	393 13.5
69.	At times he (she) feels contempt for me.	230 8.0	358 12.5	677 23.5	650 22.6	552 19.2	408 14.2
70.	Even when I can not say quite what I mean, he (she) still understands me.	364 12.5	653 22.5	825 28.4	421 14.5	338 11.6	305 10.5
71.	I think that my feeling toward him (her) helps to cause him (her) to feel the way he (she) does toward me.	379 13.0	706 24.3	908 31.3	427 14.7	257 8.8	228 7.8
72.	He (she) tries to avoid telling me anything that might upset me.	366 12.6	456 15.8	693 23.9	497 17.2	370 12.8	513 17.7

ferences in the distributions within each of the four categories. For the norm group, 19.7 per cent are $+ +$, 27.3 per cent $- +$, 31.3 per cent $+ -$, and 21.2 per cent $- -$. The private school group included 22.9 per cent $+ +$, 31.3 per cent $- +$, 28.5 per cent $+ -$, and 17.3 per cent $- -$. Thus, there were fewer people in the group who showed above average acceptance of self and more who showed acceptance of other people. In effect, the private school students said, "We are not worth as much as other people." This is often the result of living in an authority dominated world. On the other hand, these students have not rejected this authority (the authority is primarily adult, including parents, teachers and others, and church). That they have not rejected the authority is shown by the fact that fewer of them are $- -$ than in the normative group.

Other evidence of the acceptance of authority rests in the high ideal selves of these students and the low percentage of negative self-ideal discrepancies. Only 9.2 per cent of the private school students at this level were negative self-ideal discrepant. While this is a large percentage, it is not nearly so large as the 22.5 per cent of the normative group or the 30.8 per cent found in a survey of students in a large city school system made coincidentally.

Again, the scores of the girls and boys within the private school group were compared. These comparisons showed that the girls had much higher ideals than the boys, the girls had higher concepts of other people than did the boys, and girls believed that other people are more accepting of themselves than did the boys. Additionally, higher percentages of the girls were $+ +$ and $- +$ than for the boys and there were higher percentages of $+ -$ and $- -$ boys than girls. Only 6.6 percent of the girls were negative self-ideal discrepant but 12.4 per cent of the boys fell in this category.

The above data *appear* to show that the girls have healthier perceptions than the boys until it is recognized that the boys as well as the girls have above average scores on all of the variables. The differences between the boys and the girls results from the higher scores of the girls, and these scores are not always indicative of psychological health. Having high ideals is excellent except when these ideals are so high that they can never be achieved and when these ideals cause the person to see himself as inferior because he can not achieve his ideals while he believes that other people can and do. It is not healthy to aspire to be something so far beyond one's reach that frustration and feelings of inadequacy are inevitable. The high ideals of the girls approach the area of the unreachable.

High School IAV. With the exception of the school which contained grades 8-12, the High School IAV was given to all students in grades 9-12. In the exceptional case it was also given to the grade 8 students.

When the private school averages were compared with the norm averages, essentially the same picture emerged as at the junior high school level. The private school children had higher self ideals, higher concepts of other people, higher acceptance of others, and higher others possessive ideal selves. In the normative group the following percentages were in the four categories: $++$ 14.3, $-+$ 21.9, $+-$ 40.1, and $--$ 23.7. The percentages for the private school group were: $++$ 20.3, $-+$ 28.4, $+-$ 34.5, and $--$ 16.8. A big diffference between the two groups was the lower self acceptance and higher acceptance of others shown by the private school students. A second large difference in the higher ideals of the private school students and their beliefs that other people had very high ideals. The perceptions of ideals, both for self and other people, may indicate a lack of realism of these students about themselves and other people.

Again, within the private school group, boys and girls were compared for differences in responses. The girls were found to have higher self concepts, greater acceptance of self, and higher acceptance of other people. There were more $-+$ girls than boys and more $+-$ boys than girls although the differences were not great. In fact, one of the aspects of the boy-girl comparison at this level is that the great differences were not present such as were present at the junior high school level. In this respect the boys and girls at the high school level resemble those at the elementary school level. Thus, students at the elementary and high school levels are more homogeneous groups than at the junior high school level. *It also will be remembered that it is at the junior high level that the most negative attitudes toward school, the greatest authoritarianism, and the poorest teacher-student relationships existed.*

Again, at the high school level there were about twice as many boys in the negative self-ideal discrepant group as girls. The percentages were 6.4 and 3.5. For the normative group the percentage in this group is 19.6, thus, as at the junior high school level, there are far fewer negative self-ideal discrepant students in the private schools than in the public schools. The private school students trust and respect authority to a much greater degree than do the public school students. As a consequence they are probably in a poorer position to trust themselves and to exercise their own intelligence in self selected directions.

Value Differences

During 1974-75 students in a large, urban public school district were tested with the three levels of the IAV. Included were 1,854 children who completed the Elementary IAV; 1,990 who completed the Junior High IAV; and 2,154 who completed the High School IAV. In completing an IAV, students make three responses to a series of adjectives to describe themselves and three responses to describe other people. The self responses are indicators of self concept, acceptance of self, and ideal self. The others responses are indicators of the same three variables as they are perceived in other people.

The responses of the private school students and of the urban children were tabulated, item for item, and then compared to determine differences in perceptions of self and others in the two groups. This led to 111 comparisons of the High School IAV, 105 on the Junior High IAV, and 57 on the Elementary IAV for the self scales and an identical number on the others scales.

On 47 of the 57 Elementary IAV self ratings the two groups differed significantly and on 29 of the 57 others ratings the groups were significantly different. Eighty-one of the 105 self ratings on the Junior High IAV and 87 of the 105 others ratings were significantly different from each other. Of 111 self comparisons on the High School IAV, 101 were significantly different, and 99 of the 111 others comparisons were different.

These data tell two things. First, the two groups are significantly different from each other in terms of self concepts, acceptance of self, and ideals and they are likewise different in their perceptions of these characteristics in other people. Second, the higher the school level the greater is the difference between these two groups of people.

The comparisons were also examined to determine if the groups were more or less alike on self concepts and ideal self concepts, and these same two variables when used in the descriptions of other people. The Elementary IAV has 19 items. On 11 of these items the differences were greater for ideal self than for self concept and 16 were greater for others ideals than for others self concepts.

The Junior High IAV contains 35 items. Thirty-one of the 35 comparisons showed greater differences between ideal self ratings in the two groups than for self concept ratings. On 34 of the 35 comparisons, perceptions of other people's ideals showed greater differences than comparisons of other people's self concepts.

The High School IAV has 37 items. For 33 of the comparisons there was a greater difference in ideal self ratings for the two groups than for the self concept ratings. Comparisons of other people's ideals perceived by the two groups showed greater difference in 25 cases than for the corresponding comparisons of other people's self concepts.

From the above it can be concluded that not only are the two groups of people significantly different from each other in perceptions of self and of other people, but that greater difference exists in regard to ideals than in regard to self concepts, and that self ideals show greater difference between the two groups than do beliefs about the ideals of other people.

The differences in the two groups also were examined to see if generalizations could be made in regard to differences in self concepts, self acceptance, and ideal self and corresponding measures of other people, and to see if one group had higher or lower perceptions than the other.

For the Elementary IAV it could be determined that the urban group assigned itself higher ratings on 27 of the comparisons in which regular differences appeared and the private school group assigned themselves higher ratings of 21 of the comparisons in which regular differences appeared. (It should be noted in this comparison as well as in those for the Junior High and High School IAV's the number of differences is fewer than the total number of differences reported above. This is because some of the differences which were statistically significant could be interpreted as "favoring" one group or the other.) All 27 of the differences which showed higher ratings for the urban group were on self concept and acceptance of self. Fifteen of the 21 differences which favored the private school group were on ideal self ratings. Thus, the urban group described itself as having a higher self concept and greater acceptance of self while the private school group described itself as having higher ideals.

On the others form of the Elementary IAV, 11 of the differences favored the urban group and 19 favored the private school group. Of the 11 differences which favored the urban group all were on self concept and self acceptance; 15 of the 19 differences which favored the private school group were on others ideals. Thus, the urban group described other people as having higher self concepts and acceptance of self while the private school group described other people as having higher ideals.

On the Junior High IAV, the urban group assigned itself higher ratings on 24 of the 105 ratings. None of these was on a rating of the ideal self. On the other hand the private school group assigned itself 56 higher self ratings. Of the 35 items, 34 were given higher ideal self ratings by the private school group.

For others ratings on the Junior High IAV, the urban group assigned only four ratings which were higher than those assigned by the private school group. All four of these ratings were on self concept. In contrast, the private school group assigned other people 83 higher ratings. All 35 of the others ideals were higher for the private school group.

The above shows that at the Junior High level the urban and private school groups were more unlike each other than at the Elementary level. Where the urban group gave itself or other people higher ratings on the Junior High IAV, without exception these were on self concept and acceptance of self ratings. The private school group gave itself and other people higher ratings on ideals, gave itself almost as many higher self concept and self acceptance ratings as given by the urban group to itself, and saw other people having higher self concepts and acceptance of self than seen by the urban group. The two most striking differences were in the higher ideals set by the private school group for itself and the higher ratings they gave other people on all three types of ratings.

The trend shown by the differences in the Elementary IAV rat‑ ings and those of the Junior High IAV ratings continued on into the high school level. On the High School IAV the urban group gave itself only 17 of 111 ratings which were higher than those of the private school group and of these, only one was an ideal self rating. (The item is the word quiet. The private school children live in a quiet environment and desire less quiet; many of the urban school children live in a noisy environment and desire more quiet.) The private school students, though, assigned themselves 68 ratings which were higher than those assigned by the urban group to itself. Of the 68 ratings, only two were on self acceptance, 30 were on self concept, and 36 were on ideal self. In other words, the private schools did not show high acceptance of themselves but did have high self concepts and even higher ideal selves.

Practically the same picture was shown by the others ratings on the High School IAV. The urban group gave other people 12 ratings which were higher than those given by the private school group; none of these were on ideals. The private school group gave other people 69 higher ratings and all 37 traits showed higher ideals.

Thus, the private and urban groups were significantly different from each other in self concepts, acceptance of self, and ideal self and in their perceptions of other people. The data show, also, that the higher the school group the more it differs from its counterpart. The greatest difference between the two groups is in ideals—both those they seek for themselves and those they believe are held by other people. The private school students appear to be striving for perfection and believe that to a large degree other people have achieved it.

The above picture is consistent with personal observations of the students. On the average, the private school students appeared to be conservative of dress and appearance. They were quite, neat, and "mannerly."

5

How Headmasters
Rate Teachers

Each headmaster was asked to rate the effectiveness of each teacher on a seven point scale. The points on the scale were: exceptional, good, above average, average, below average, poor, and unacceptable. Values of one through seven are assigned these ratings with one representing exceptional and seven representing unacceptable.

The 206 teachers who were given ratings by their headmasters had an average rating of 2.5 which places them half-way between good and above average. In the large urban study which supplied the IAV data used in the previous section, 1,461 teachers were rated by the principals and achieved an average rating of 2.6; about the same as that for the private school teachers.

The above averages do not describe the entire situation. In most of the private schools one or more of the teachers was reported as being a serious problem and disrupting influence. The public schools have their own disrupters. However, the situation differs markedly. The median number of teachers in the 11 private schools which were studied was 18; the range varied from 8 in the school which contained only grades 8-12 to 45 in the largest school. The average public school has more than 18 teachers; thus, the ineffective may be more diluted and less disruptive than in the private schools.

In examining the above average, it is important to remember

that the ratings given each of the groups may not be comparable. When ratings are examined school by school for either the private school group or the urban school system, it is obvious that principals use different criteria in different schools—some principals give high ratings to most of their teachers, other give low ratings to most of the teachers.

6

Teachers' Perceptions of
Their Problems

Each teacher was asked to sort the 84 problems of the Teacher Problems Q-Sort. These problems are representative of the problems which teachers encounter in their teaching. In making a sort, a teacher places the 84 problems in 11 categories which represent a normal distribution, placing the most pressing problems at one end of the distribution and the least pressing ones at the other end.

These problems may be scored to give a measure of the openness of teachers to their experience. Previous research has shown that the openness of teachers is related to their teaching effectiveness. Openness to experience is a personality construct in which a teacher who is open has available to him, without distortion or denial, his past experience to serve as a basis for present behavior. If the teacher is less open, his experience is denied and/or distorted and he has less than an adequate basis for his behavior. The less open teacher is defensive and defends himself against change.

The problems of an open teacher are characterized by positive attitudes toward self and other people, by a concern for central issues rather than peripheral ones, by centering the locus of responsibility for doing something about the problem within himself rather than outside himself or in other people, by reflecting the inclusion of self in the problem or its solution, by concern for the future rather than concern only for the past and/or present. Thus, problems can become a means of understanding the openness of teachers. Open teachers, in addition to other characteristics maintain more helpful relationships with their students; they are seen by their students as more positive in their regard, as more empathic in their understanding, as less conditional in their regard, and as more congruent.

To illustrate how openness qualities are shown by problems, two examples will be cited. In the first example, the most pressing problem of a teacher might be, "Teaching children who lack the desire to learn." This is a problem of a less open teacher since the problem implies a negative attitude toward the children (they do not desire to learn), it does not involve the self of the teacher, the time orientation is in the present and does not reflect the future, responsibility for change is the students' and not the teacher's since the students will have to change for the problem to be solved, and the problem is probably peripheral with the central issue being the teacher's concern that the students are not learning as he thinks they should.

A problem for the more open teacher would be the one which states, "How to become the most positive educational influence in the lives of my students that I can be." The problem is central, it involves the teacher in its solution, the attitude of the teacher is positive, and it is oriented toward the future.

The average score on the Teacher Problems Q-Sort which was established by prior research is 5.2. In contrast, the average score of the teachers in the private schools was 8.1. Thus, the average teacher in the private schools was more open to experience than the average teacher in the public schools.

When the averages were computed for each of the schools, it was found that they ranged from .8 to 13.5 which meant that the schools differed significantly from each other. The average for the school with the large, beautiful campus described earlier in this report was 12.2 which places it next to the highest and the average for the garment factory school was 6.3 which placed it next to the lowest.

A measure of the accuracy with which the problems were sorted in each school was computed. This average showed wide variation among the schools. The least accurate was the garment factory school and the most accurate was the school with the large, beautiful campus.

A composite description of all of the problems was constructed. This composite showed that the most pressing problem was "helping children to learn to think for themselves and to be independent." The next most important problems were "how to make the subject matter interesting and meaningful to all pupils of varying ability," and "how to develop responsibility of pupils for their behavior." It is interesting to note that all three of these problems are those of the open teacher. It is also interesting to note, that according to the findings from the Locus of Responsibility Scale, that the teachers' behavior toward students is inconsistent with the goals stated in these problems. It will be remembered that teachers in the private schools made more than the average number of decisions for their students and tended to dominate them. However, when information from the Index of Adjustment and Values is included, it probably is not true that the teachers are seen by the students as authoritarians. Instead, these students expect adults to be more authoritative and do not reject their authority.

It is clear that based on the Teacher Problems Q-Sort, the teachers in the private schools are more open to their experience.

7

Another Look

Eleven private schools volunteered to participate in the study. All generalizations about the schools must be qualified by the manner in which they were selected, the size of the sample, and other important considerations. Based on observations, information provided by the headmasters, and the objective instruments used in the study, it is obvious that the 11 private schools are different from each other and conclusions which overlook these differences are not warranted. However, some significant generalizations can be made.

These private schools operate under severe handicaps. They frequently have an insufficient pool of children from which to draw to assure adequate financial support, inadequately prepared teachers, weak headmasters who lack training and experience in administrative roles, and a restricted curriculum. Serious problems are posed for parents forming one of these schools in accumulating construction, operational and maintenance financing. Usually, funds are insufficient for an adequate and minimally equipped school plant, quality teachers, instructional and other supplies, and to provide a quality learning program.

Teacher and headmaster turn-over is high from year to year. The headmaster may receive the brunt of the parents' frustrations and may not be prepared adequately to cope with these problems and those associated with the development of a new educational enterprise. Teacher turn-over is high because of low salaries and the ineptitude of some of the teachers.

Although most of these schools begin as an effort to avoid problems brought on by the changing nature of the public schools, they seldom continue to exist for these same reasons. After formation, the purposes of the schools tend toward providing a "Christian" education and/or providing a quality education usually designed to prepare students for college. Unfortunately, the schools seldom reach the goal of providing a quality education. Other things being equal, the longer a school has been in existence the more quality it may have. However, a large number of these schools fail to survive the initial three or four year period required to construct the building, employ teachers, attain financial stability, assure minimal equipment, and develop at least a minimal curriculum. No accurate data are available regarding rate of failure of these schools but the number appears to be high.

Due to inadequate finances, libraries are poor, lunch programs are highly inadequate, and transportation is poorly organized. In all but one school the lunch program consisted of hot and cold sandwiches sold either by the school or catering organizations. Each of these schools, with one exception, has numerous Coke and potato chip vending machines. Little attention is given to milk; instead children often drink Cokes.

Vending machines are sometimes big business in these schools. One school reported that its machines grossed $25,000 during 1973-74. The full time of one woman is taken up with replenishing the machines after the pre-school rush to ready them for the mid-morning break and the lunchtime onslaught. This woman reports that many of the children arrive at school without breakfast, since their mothers work and leave home before the children get ready for school in the morning. She said, "It's a matter of values. If you want your child to have a good Christian education such as they get here, both parents have to work. You have to decide if you want your child to have a good breakfast or a good Christian education."

In another school, vending machines are operated by local vendors who sometimes supply a cafeteria worker to make change, and for the small children, to operate the microwave oven and to open the cans of heated food. (It was distressing to see the children hanging on the microwave oven as it operated.) In another school the "cafeteria" is 'a modern, soda-fountain-like building which is housed behind the school building. This "cafeteria" provides the full array of food and goods found in the usual soda-fountain, drug store luncheonette except that it does not serve plate lunches. The building is leased to and operated by the state commission for the blind.

These schools are costly. The average parent pays a stiff price for what is offered. Although these schools are in a position to make contributions to the education of their children because of the absence of restricting state limitations, they do not capitalize on their opportunities. *Instead, they are inferior copies of traditional practices which are rapidly being abandoned by the public schools.*

Other limitations of the schools are the lack of health care facilities and personnel, special personnel such as librarians and counselors, and absence of testing programs to assess pupil needs and with which to evaluate the effectiveness of the schools in reaching their goals. Because of the costs, the schools are unable to meet the minimum accreditation standards of regional accrediting agencies and substitute, instead, the highly inadequate standards of their own accrediting agencies.

In spite of the above dismal picture, the parents have strong positive attitudes toward these schools. The schools offer solutions to problems which the parents believe would be catastrophic for their children. They own the schools and have pride in the ownership. (Since they pay "double taxation" in their own eyes—supporting the public schools and the private schools, too—they must rationalize that they are receiving their money's worth. At the same time they deeply resent the need for supporting two school systems.) Furthermore, the strained human relationships and serious discipline problems which are frequent in the public schools virtually are absent in these private schools. A most important factor in the attitudes of the parents is the responsiveness of the schools to their opinions and wishes. The schools can exist only if all parents continue to give their support, and the loss of even one child is felt in meeting payrolls, mortgage payments, and other bills. The public schools could learn from these schools the value of parent involvement and of being responsive to the parents. Instead, far too often public school parents do not believe that they own the schools or that the schools are influenced by their thoughts and desires.

If the morality of people is classed in three categories—preconventional, conventional, and principled—the private school parents are seen to be operating at the level of conventional morality. In preconventional morality, it will be recalled, the person responds in terms of "what's in it for me" meaning that sometimes he responds in terms of the rewards or punishments he will receive and at other times in terms of mutual accommodation. At the conventional level, the person responds in terms of "absolutes" or of moral values which usually have not grown from personal experience but have been imposed from outside the person by the home, the church, the school, or otherwise. At the principled level, the person's values have grown from his own experience; they are a part of him and it becomes easier for him to decide how he should behave.

Since the parents of the private school children exist at a conventional morality level, they seek "Christian" education for their children or they seek to give their children an education which is consistent with the American way of life—which also is seen as a "Christian" way of life.

In most public schools, parent attitudes toward the schools becomes less positive as the children move to the higher grades. Although the same is true for the private schools included in this study, it is not true to the same extent and at no level of the school can parents' attitudes be classed as negative.

The students also experience positive attitudes toward the private schools. Their attitudes toward the schools vary from school to school, as might be expected, and in some of the schools the average student attitude is below the norm average whereas in other schools it is far above the average. Boys' attitudes toward the schools, as in the public schools, are less positive than those of the girls. However, the average for the boys in the private schools is above that of all of the students in the public schools. Although students' attitudes toward the public schools decline from grade four through grade 12, the same is not true in these private schools. The low point, from the students' point of view, is grade 8. They feel more positively about the school before this point and will feel more positively about it later. It is in the junior high school grades that these children appear to be moving from the more concrete conventional morality of younger children to the more abstract conventional morality of their high school peers. During this period, there is considerably more difficulty in teachers relating successfully to the students.

The teachers in these private schools are characterized as young, minimally prepared, with little teaching experience. They often teach burdensome loads to a broad variety of age and interest levels within a single classroom and often teach in fields in which they have had little, if any, preparation. The teachers probably are characterized by a high level of conventional morality which expresses itself in relationships which are characterized by teacher domination and conditionality of regard. The teachers are more authoritative and direct than their peers in the public schools. Yet they are probably not seen as authoritarian by the students. These students expect adults and people in positions of leadership to provide a strong hand in showing them the direction in which they should move. Even though they may not like this type of relationship, they accept it as natural and do not question the authority of the teachers or of the schools.

As in the public schools, teachers are more direct in their relationships with boys than with girls, more frequently telling the boys what they must do and interacting with girls in deciding what will be done. The amount of teacher-made decisions was low in grades 4-6 but increased significantly in grades 7 and 8. From grade 8 through grade 12 there was a regular decline. Interaction of teachers with students showed the opposite. Interaction as a means of making decisions in the classroom decreased through grade 8 and then increased regularly from grade 9 through grade 12. The shift in attitude of students toward the school closely parallels the change in the locus of decision making within the classrooms.

The quality of relationships between teacher and student in the private school is superior to that in public schools. The greatest differences are in level of regard, a measure of the importance the students have for the teacher, and congruence which is a measure of the openness of the teacher in the relationship with the students. In regard to congruence, in these private schools, as in public schools, teachers are more congruent in their relationships with girls than with boys, however, the difference in the private schools is greater than in the public schools.

Although differences in relationship qualities are not present among the grades in the public schools, they are present in the private schools. These trends duplicate those found in the students' attitudes and in the locus of decision making. Why these same differences appear on all three of the measures used for these assessments is not known. It is clear, though, that in some significant respect the students and/or the goals of the teachers are significantly different in the private and public schools. The resulting situation is far from wholesome when the children's developing attitudes toward self and others and their developing values are considered.

The study shows that the private school children do not perceive themselves as having as much worth as children in the public schools. They underrate themselves and overrate other people. A second important difference in the private school children is that they set much higher ideals for themselves than do public school children and they believe that other people have even higher ideals. Furthermore, when private school boys and girls are compared it is found that the girls underrate themselves more than do the boys, they overrate other people more than do the boys, they set higher ideals for themselves, and they believe that other people have higher ideals.

The most notable difference in personal characteristics between the public school and private school students relates to the higher ideals of the children in the private schools. These high ideals clearly mark the children's morality as conventional. Their ideals are so high that they will lead to frustrations and anxiety and cause the students to be classed as strivers and probably as compulsive strivers when they become adults.

On the basis of self and others perceptions, the public and private school students represent two distinctly different groups. *One of the most significant aspects of the difference is the greater conventional morality of the private school children and the higher preconventional morality of the public school children.* Since there are few children in any schools with principled morality this aspect of the comparison has little significance.

There is little evidence to suggest that schools (public or private) have any significant success in moral or character development. Quite likely the differences observed in the private school students did not develop in their private schools but as a result of home and church environment and other influences. It is known, though, that children change under peer pressure. If the private school children were placed in public schools where they were in the majority, they might exert a positive influence on the other students. However, in the areas where the private schools have developed, the children usually constitute a minority in their public schools and the direction of change would be for at least some of the private school children to give up their conventional morality without adequate substitutes for it. While conventional morality has numerous harmful side effects for the person and for other people in contact with him, it has less harmful ones than those of preconventional morality.

It is highly likely that if the private school children were to be placed in public schools where they are in the minority they would be overwhelmed by the differences in morality and would change toward greater preconventional morality. Again, although conventional morality is not the most desirable state of affairs, preconventional morality is even less desirable.

The above argument sounds strangely like that given by the parents as reasons for forming private schools. The parents contend that their children are different from a large proportion of the public school children. In that belief they are correct as shown by the results of the study. Furthermore, it appears that forcing these children to attend the public schools would not be helpful to them and probably would not be helpful to the other children. These children accept and respect authority. They seek for an absolute type of morality and these beliefs can be destroyed with rapidity as shown by recent nationwide trends. It is interesting to note that parents do not form the type of private school included in this study or begin sending their children in large numbers to the ones which exist until their children become the minority group within a school or until it is anticipated that they will become a minority group. The school with the

181

large, beautiful campus, described earlier in this report, developed rapidly when the city school system faced court-ordered massive integration of the races and the parents who elected to send their children to the private school were those in school zones which would be faced with the largest amounts of integration. Another of the schools struggled to establish itself until the ratio of black/white students in the public school passed the magical 50 per cent tilt level. At that point the parents enrolled their children in the private school. In another instance the private school was not formed when the schools were integrated but was formed after the court demanded equalization of the black:white ratio throughout the county school system which was predominantly black, and massive bussing was required to achieve it.

An interesting side effect appears in the private schools in regard to the openness and effectiveness of the teachers. As stated above, on the average the teachers are minimally prepared (some do not even reach the minimum of a bachelor's degree), young, and inexperienced. They are directive with their students and are conditional in their expression of regard for the students which is at least partially a reflect of their lack of experience and their own conventional morality. Under these conditions it would be expected that both parents and students would not hold positive attitudes toward the schools. To the contrary, though, both parents and students hold positive attitudes. Very likely this is the result of an authority dominated culture. The parents believe that they should exercise authority over their children and the children both accept and respect this authority. They feel the same way in regard to their churches and it is only a natural extension to the teacher-student relationship. Thus, the students accept the authority of the teachers without question and without resentment. The students in such authority situations as those presented by the home, church, and school which are characterized by conditional regard, react by questioning their own worth, accepting other people as having more worth than they, setting high conventional values, and believing that other people have at least equally high conventional values.

A direct consequence of the above is that these minimally qualified and poorly experienced teachers are rated as successful in their teaching as a group of more highly prepared and experienced teachers in a large urban school district which was used for comparison purposes. A second consequence is that the private school teachers are more open to their experiencing than the more experienced urban teachers. Prior study has indicated that inexperienced and poorly qualified teachers are defensive in their classroom behavior. As a consequence they are less open to experience. The private schools, though, do not offer teachers threatening interpersonal relationships with students since the students are ready and willing to accept the authority of the teachers. In a public school classroom these inexperienced teachers probably would be far less open to their experience.

It is interesting to speculate about the possible consequences of public school experience on children with the value systems and respect for authority such as those who attend the private schools. Given a lower level of authority and a higher level of opportunity to accept responsibility for themselves such as is presented in many public school classrooms (especially in the lower grades), these children would tend to over-react to their newly found liberty and to become discipline problems (not of a delinquent type but that which would be characterized by being late to classes, coming to school poorly prepared, procrastination in assignments, and other such behavior). Experienced teachers are able to avoid these problems by gradually relinquishing more and more authority to the children. Unfortunately, this is more the case in the elementary schools than in the curriculum-centered secondary schools where the textbook is more often the authority.

The qualitative and descriptive data indicate that the private schools which were studied should be of a highly inferior quality as measured by their effects on the children but the quantitative data suggest that the results are not entirely as expected and that for the children in these private schools, experience in their public schools might have highly undesirable consequences. Further study is needed to determine the amount of cognitive achievement of the children in the private schools. The inadequate data which are available suggest that cognitive achievement may be about the same for the private schools as for the public schools (contrary to the claims of the schools and the hopes of the parents), but questions about cognitive achievement can be answered only through a survey in which the achievement of the children in the 11 schools of the study could be measured with standardized tests using the same instruments in all of the schools and at the same grade levels.

Index